Nonviolence. A Quick Immersion

Quick Immersions use accurate and straightforward language to offer a good introduction, or deeper knowledge, on diverse issues. Well structured texts by prestigious authors, they delve into the worlds of political and social science, philosophy, hard science and the humanities.

Andrew Fiala

NONVIOLENCE
A Quick Immersion

Tibidabo Publishing
New York

Contents

List of illustrations

Preface

As I complete this book, a wave of nonviolent social protest has erupted across the United States in response to racism and police brutality. The commonly used name for this nonviolent movement is Black Lives Matter. The movement began as three women —Alicia Garza, Patrisse Cullors, and Opal Tometi— channeled their outrage at Black Americans being killed by police and racist vigilantes. They created a nonviolent campaign to demand the end of this kind of violence. The names of the victims who inspired Black Lives Matter, when it began in 2013, include Trayvon Martin, Michael Brown, and Eric Garner. Before them, there is a long line of Black victims of violence including Rodney King, Emmet Till, and others who were lynched, beaten, and murdered. In 2020, the names of Ahmaud Arbery, Breonna Taylor, and George Floyd were added to this appalling list of victims.

While there has been some looting and violence during the protests of 2020, the lasting image is of the police violently assaulting nonviolent protestors. Crowds of nonviolent protesters have been teargassed, shot at with rubber bullets, and arrested. This has included journalists, who have been assaulted and arrested. In Buffalo, New York, a 75-year-old nonviolent protester, Martin Gugino, was shoved to the ground by police, which cracked his skull. He was left bleeding on the sidewalk as the police marched by. In Washington, D.C., security forces used gas and flash grenades to clear nonviolent protesters out of Lafayette Park so that President Trump could stand in front of St. John's Episcopal Church, as part of the President's effort to demonstrate his power and strength. These assaults by security forces inadvertently demonstrate the power of nonviolence. As the state becomes more brutal in its effort to suppress nonviolent protest, sympathy for the protesters grows and the forces of repression look increasingly morally bankrupt. This is how and why nonviolence works. It does not always work. But the protests of 2020 provide a lesson in the power of nonviolence.

Some critics have responded to Black Lives Matter by claiming that "all lives matter" (and defenders of the police have also insisted that "blue lives matter"). It is true that all lives matter. And, in fact, Black Lives Matter has included a conscious effort to be inclusive that is informed by what scholars call "intersectionality", a commitment to deep diversity that includes the concerns of women, members of LGBTQ communities, and so on. But when some people's lives are viewed as having less value than others (as is true of Black people in the United States), it is necessary to insist on a special focus on the value of those lives. Nonetheless, the fundamental moral principle here is the idea that life itself matters. This is the basic intuition of nonviolence. Albert Schweitzer identified this as the basic principle of ethics: "It is good to maintain and encourage life; it is bad to destroy life or to obstruct it". This moral intuition is central to the long history of nonviolence. This tradition begins from Socrates, Jesus, and the Buddha. It includes more contemporary figures such as Mohandas K Gandhi, Martin Luther King Jr., Desmond Tutu, and the Dalai Lama. Nonviolent movements for social change have made profound and lasting impacts on the world. They continue to be powerful because of their internal consistency and integrity. By avoiding violence and remaining committed to truth, justice, and love, we demonstrate the value of a theory and practice that affirms life.

Chapter 1

Introduction

We are making progress towards a less violent world. Even before the emergence of nonviolent protests against racism and police brutality in 2020, scholars had argued that we are in the midst of one of the largest waves of nonviolent mass movements in history. Across the globe, people are taking to the streets, to social media, and to the courts. There are still acts of terrorism, crime, and police brutality. Governments still oppress their people. Military and police forces still use excessive violence. But the idea that social protest — and life itself — ought to be nonviolent has caught on. And as new waves of nonviolence emerge, they are informed by the history of nonviolence and facilitated by new strategies made possible by emerging technologies —including especially social media, which allows for quick and efficient organization of mass protests and demonstrations.

Even though the technology changes, the value of nonviolence remains the same. Nonviolence is strategic use of constructive force to build a world of human flourishing. Nonviolence is affirmative and positive: it aims to create without destroying. Nonviolence includes a critique of the destructive force of violence. But it is not simply a critical or negative doctrine: it is a method of building, creating, and constructing. In nonviolence, means and ends are interconnected. Nonviolence uses truthful, just, and loving means to cultivate peaceful outcomes that are also characterized by love, truth, and justice.

There is persuasive power in nonviolence, perhaps even coercive power. A nonviolent protest is intended to force a change. But unlike violence, nonviolence is not primarily focused on power or domination. It does not view power as an end in itself. The power associated with nonviolence is not brute strength, supremacy, dominance, or hierarchical authority. While violence destroys and threatens destruction, nonviolence builds through affirmation and consent. Its power is related to the uplifting value of both its means and its ends. It is persuasive because of the integrity and rationality of its goals and its methods. Nonviolence does not aim to destroy or dominate an opponent. Rather,

(margin handwritten note: violence doesn't solve the issue to protect human being)

its goal is transformation and growth. This is more like education than extermination. It is more like discussion than debate. It is more like giving birth than demanding submission.

Some consider nonviolence merely as a pragmatic method for producing social change. Others are committed to nonviolence as a moral principle. And some think of nonviolence as the basis for a way of life. But the shared idea is that nonviolence is both moral and effective. Nonviolence has been employed in successful campaigns of social change. It has a deep history, connected to important sources in morality and religion. And there is a contemporary theory that justifies and explains how and why it works.

Methods of Nonviolent Protest

Nonviolent protest involves a number of strategies. Gene Sharp famously listed 198 different methods of nonviolent action. This list ranges from making public speeches and writing letters to creating alternative political structures. The list includes various forms of strikes, boycotts, and demonstrations. Sharp broadly identifies three types of nonviolent action:

- Symbolic protest and persuasion (for example, letter writing);
- Non-cooperation (for example, work slow-downs); and
- Intervention (for example, civil disobedience).

These methods overlap and intermingle. Coordinated nonviolent campaigns employ and adopt multiple techniques, often dividing up the labor among a cohort of activists: some write letters, some coordinate strikes and boycotts, others participate in civil disobedience. Social movements also employ a coordinated strategy involving both institutional and extra-institutional means: some run for office or file lawsuits, others walk picket lines or get arrested during protests. The fact that there is such an array of techniques, methods, tactics, and strategies provides a rejoinder to those who suggest that nonviolence is weak and useless. Nonviolent political action is complex, multi-faceted, and adaptable. And it is often effective. For more discussion of methods, strategies, and techniques see Chapter 4.

Nonviolence continues to grow and develop in both theory and practice. The philosophy of nonviolence includes deep reflection on ethics, human nature, religion, and political philosophy. Sometimes this theoretical focus is moralistic: some dogmatically insist that nonviolence is the best or only way forward. But there are also empirical studies of effective nonviolence and a corresponding critical analysis of violence. These empirical studies form the root of "peace studies" or what is sometimes called "peace and conflict studies". A robust and comprehensive philosophy of nonviolence combines the empirical study of nonviolent conflict resolution with a normative critique of violence. This book considers both empirical and normative issues, while also discussing how nonviolence seeks to transform our thinking about self, world, and meaning. After reading it, you will understand *what* nonviolence is, *why* nonviolence should be valued, and *how* nonviolence ought to be practiced. We will also discuss the question of *who* practices nonviolence and *to whom* nonviolence ought to be directed. Along the way we will discuss key figures in the tradition of nonviolence.

A Brief History of Nonviolence

Mohandas K. Gandhi and Martin Luther King Jr. are well-known as advocates of nonviolence. The Reverend Martin Luther King Jr. said, "Nonviolence is a powerful and just weapon. It is a weapon unique in history, that cuts without wounding and ennobles the man who wields it. It is a sword that heals". King developed his thinking from studying Mahatma Gandhi (*mahatma* means "great soul"—it is not Gandhi's first name!). Gandhi himself said, "nonviolence is the way to freedom —not the forced non-violence of the slave, but the willing non-violence of the brave and the free". These are inspiring words. But what does it mean to say that nonviolence is a sword that heals, a just weapon of the free and the brave? This book seeks to answer that question.

Gandhi and King did not invent nonviolence. The history of nonviolence is ancient and global. It was proposed in various ways by Jesus, Socrates, the Buddha, and Mahavira (the founder of Jainism). The basic idea is that constructive power that avoids violence is the higher, more enlightened, and more ethical path. Gandhi's work grew out of South Asian religions such as Jainism, Buddhism, and Hinduism. He worked with Muslims who also advocated for nonviolence. Gandhi also knew of varieties of Christian nonviolence. In the Christian world, there is a tradition of nonviolence found especially among Quakers, Mennonites, and other Anabaptists. In the U.S., in the middle part of the twentieth century, King offered a further synthesis that more closely linked Gandhian ideas to Christian thinking. But King was not alone in his work. The history of nonviolence in the U.S. includes such key figures as Richard Gregg, A.J. Muste, James Lawson, Cesar Chavez, Dorothy Day, and others. Soon we will be adding to this list the organizers and theorists who are leading Black Lives Matter protests, as well as others from across the globe.

One of Gandhi's influences was the Russian author Leo Tolstoy. Tolstoy was himself influenced by American transcendentalist author Henry David Thoreau. In his 1848 essay "On Civil Disobedience", Thoreau imagined conscientious people organizing themselves, refusing allegiance to unjust laws, and changing political reality through what he called

[handwritten margin note: nonviolence is more logical than violence]

everyone is equal and governed [handwritten marginal note]

civil disobedience [handwritten annotation]

"a peaceable revolution". Thoreau's thinking was in turn influenced by the Anglo-American tradition of democratic politics, which holds that laws ought to be both equitable and just, that persons are created equal, and that political power rests upon the consent of the governed. Thoreau was also influenced by the tradition of Christian pacifism, what was often called "nonresistance" in the nineteenth century. While some forms of nonresistance focus primarily on an individual's refusal to cooperate, a more developed notion of nonviolent social protest aims to stimulate social change by mobilizing mass movements. For Christians, the nonviolent ideal grows from basic principles found in the Christian gospels: that we ought to turn the other cheek, that we should not return evil for evil, and that we ought to love our neighbors and our enemies.

The method of nonviolent civil disobedience advocated by Thoreau also has deep roots. Protestants in Europe, for example, were those who "protested" against the Catholic faith, often in nonviolent ways. Martin Luther —the namesake of Martin Luther King Jr.— engaged in an act of nonviolent civil disobedience when he nailed his 95 Theses to the door in Wittenberg. A similar method was employed by American colonists during the famous Boston Tea Party. Gandhi developed these strategies further, showing that a coordinated campaign of nonviolence could be effective. This method has been developed further and supplemented by new and emerging technologies. Luther's hammer gave way to Gandhi's marches, which has in turn been supplemented by social media and global cellphone communication. There have also been empirical studies showing how and why nonviolence works in struggles for democracy and human rights.

The message of nonviolence has by now become commonplace and has gained adherents everywhere. The Dalai Lama, for example, has repeatedly called for nonviolence —even in his struggle against the Chinese occupation of Tibet. He wrote in 1999:

> If we look at history, we find that in time, humanity's love of peace, justice, and freedom always triumphs over cruelty and oppression. This is why I am such a fervent believer in nonviolence. Violence begets violence. And violence only means one thing: suffering.

More recently the Dalai Lama explained, "One of the most important ancient Indian ideas is 'ahimsa,' non-violence, which I consider to be compassion in action. It doesn't mean weakness, cowering in fear, or simply doing nothing. It is to act without violence, recognizing the rights of others".

A similar sentiment has been expressed by Pope Francis. On January 1, 2017 on World Peace Day, Pope Francis gave an address entitled "Nonviolence: A Style of Politics for Peace". He reminded the world that nonviolence was the message preached by Jesus: "Jesus marked out the path of nonviolence". Francis called on Catholics to engage in "peacebuilding through active nonviolence". He concluded his address, saying, "may we dedicate ourselves prayerfully and actively to banishing violence from our hearts, words and deeds, and to becoming nonviolent people and to building nonviolent communities that care for our common home".

In his speech, Pope Francis celebrated Mother Theresa, Mohandas K. Gandhi, Martin Luther King Jr., Khan Abdul Ghaffar Khan, and Leymah Gbowee as heroes of nonviolence. Francis might have included a long list of others. For example, he might have cited Malala Yousafzai, a Pakistani girl who was shot in the head by Taliban terrorists in Pakistan in 2012 for speaking out in defense of education for girls. Malala survived the attack. She went on to become an international voice advocating for nonviolence, education, and rights for women. She was the youngest person ever to receive the Nobel Peace Prize. In the summer of 2013, when she was just 16 years old, she gave an address to the United Nations, where she listed her personal influences, including: the prophet Muhmmad, Jesus, the Buddha, Martin Luther King, Nelson Mandela, Muhammad Ali Jinnah, Gandhi, Bacha Khan, and Mother Teresa. She said, "this is what my soul is telling me, be peaceful and love everyone".

All of this reminds us that nonviolence is a truly global philosophy with adherents from multiple traditions including Islam, Christianity, Hinduism, *is for everyone*

Buddhism, and so on. There is a global sense of nonviolence that is important for people across the globe and from all cultures. We continue to see nonviolent social protest break out across the globe. And although nonviolent action is not a panacea that works in every case, there is a long history of successful nonviolent actions. Gandhi's work for Indian liberation provides one example. The U.S. Civil Rights movement provides another. Since the 1960's, there have been nonviolent actions in Europe, Africa, Asia, and Latin America. Sometimes these actions have been brutally repressed —as in the aftermath of the so-called "Arab Spring" of the past decade. But often nonviolence has proved to be what Peter Ackerman and Jack DuVall call "a force more powerful". Consider the successful nonviolent campaigns we have witnessed, among others: those movements that brought about the demise of Soviet-style governments in Central and Eastern Europe and the fall of the Berlin Wall; struggles for power in Latin American countries such as Chile that continue today; protests against authoritarian governments in Africa and the Middle East (including the movement to dismantle South Africa's apartheid regime, as well as the "Arab Spring" and the Palestinian Intifada); the struggle for autonomy in Hong Kong, and so on. Political action across the globe continues to employ and develop nonviolent techniques: in environmental movements, feminist movements, and movements for social justice. *bringing justice and equality to all*

1. Protester holding a Malala Yousafza banner during a protest to support her.

The effort to change society without violence continues to inspire the work of activists across the globe in conjunction with a variety of issues from protests against racism, police brutality, and political repression to demonstrations in support of action to prevent climate change, in defense of women's rights, and in opposition to rapacious capitalism. In what follows we will consider these efforts and think critically about the value and power of nonviolence, while considering how the advocates of nonviolence understand themselves and the world around them.

Chapter 2

What is Nonviolence?

The theory and practice of nonviolence has often included an extensive critique of violence. But this critical focus often distracts from the affirmative and positive heart of nonviolence. Nonviolence can be understood in positive terms as the strategic use of constructive force to build a world of human flourishing. We might define nonviolence in positive terms as humane-ness, compassion, or lovingkindness. Violence is a significant problem for the actualization of kindness, justice, and constructive force. But the positive vision of nonviolence is not only concerned with rejecting violence, it is also concerned with building, loving, and empathizing with others.

The term "nonviolence" usually does not stand alone as a concept or value. Rather, it is often used as an adjective to describe something else. Thus we speak of nonviolent social protest, nonviolent communication, nonviolent policing, nonviolent parenting, and nonviolent agriculture. When activities are nonviolent, they avoid deliberately harming others and seek to actualize kindness, justice, creativity, and love.

Most discussions of nonviolence focus primarily on nonviolent social activism or nonviolent political movements. This is creative and non-destructive power applied to political and social activity. We might even also speak of "nonviolent coercion" here. While this sounds like an oxymoron, it is actually what many of the most famous advocates of nonviolent social protest have in mind. Nonviolent social protest seeks to persuade and convert opponents. There is an element of coercion in social and political activism. The point of a strike or a boycott or a campaign of civil disobedience is to force the opponent to respond. The "force" that is used here is nonviolent: no one is physically harmed and there is hope for a creative and positive resolution.

Like other important ideas, nonviolence is complex. Nonviolence has been qualified and described in various ways. Martin Luther King Jr., reminds us that there is a difference between those who adopt nonviolence as a technique or strategy and those who understand it as a "way of life". The idea of nonviolence as a way of life is connected to the idealism of what we might call "pacifism" (a term that is also subject to varying interpretations). Within the domain of strategic nonviolence, various terms have been employed: civil resistance, popular resistance, people power, and even passive resistance. The latter term is misleading insofar as nonviolence is usually not "passive". Strategic nonviolence is politically focused, non-institutional, and forceful. It also often operates outside of conventional legal and political frameworks. But we should note that democratic politics contains a crucial element of nonviolence: democratic electoral systems allow for nonviolent transfers of power; and the norms of liberal-democratic politics generally focus on nonviolent conflict resolution.

The term nonviolence is most obviously understood as the negation of violence. But this way of understanding nonviolence is both unfortunate and uninformative. It is unfortunate because as a negative term, the term "nonviolence" contains the very thing it rejects. This terminological difficulty afflicts the philosophy of nonviolence, which strikes some as a negative and even reactionary idea. Critics will even claim that it is a kind of cowardice or fear of violence. They will suggest that advocates of nonviolence do nothing or are unwilling to do what is necessary to promote social change. In response, defenders of nonviolence argue that nonviolence is not merely negative:

there are lots of things that nonviolent activists do to promote social change.

The terminological problem shows up in many languages. In the languages and cultures of South Asia —in the traditions of Hinduism, Jainism, Buddhism, and in the philosophy of Mohandas K. Gandhi— the term *ahimsa* is employed. This term is also a negative one: *a-himsa* (non-violence) is the negation of *himsa* (violence). In Spanish, the term is *la no-violencia*. In French, the term is *la non-violence*. In German, two related terms are used to translate nonviolence: *Gewaltlosigkeit* (which means without violence) and *Gewaltfreiheit* (which means free of violence). The German language is provocative here, offering us the idea of being free of violence. This helps us imagine a variety of other formulations in English, including: "violence-free action", "violence-less-ness", or "action-without-violence". Of course, those formulations still contain the term violence and still suggest something negative. Other related terms are also negative in their formulation: non-harming, non-injury, or non-killing. These terms seek to fill in some content to the idea of violence: identifying violence as harm or injury —or more specifically as killing. These clarifications are useful. A theory of non-harming, for example, connects with the central idea in medical ethics (and in other fields) that we must first "do no harm". Non-injury is a term that makes us think of health as its opposite: a "non-injured" organ, for example, is healthy and functions normally. The negative formulation implies that in order to be free of violence or harm we must somehow escape from or negate violence. And indeed, there have been various proposals for how this can be done, as we shall see.

But the terminological complications continue. Nonviolence may be connected with "anti-violence" or "counter-violence". Anti-violence often means taking action to oppose violence, as when a protest movement forms against rape or guns. A movement that aims to reduce violence against women would be an "anti-violence" movement, as would a movement in favor of gun control. Counter-violence often means the use of violence by the police or a "peace-keeping force" that uses violence to prevent or limit violence. The theory and practice of nonviolence is indeed anti-violence. But it generally does not seek to employ counter-violence. Instead, nonviolent theory and practice seeks to limit violence by turning away from violence. This could be related to a focus on a wide range of "un-violent" activities: eating, sleeping, making love, making art, doing science, and thinking about philosophy. But un-violence does not seem to capture what we have in mind when we think of nonviolent protest, which is an action that includes a social and political agenda for change and which involves the use of persuasive force and coercive (but nonviolent) power. And yet, some of the methods of nonviolent social protest are essentially "un-violent". These are the methods of *noncooperation* including: staying home from work and school, boycotting businesses and events, work slow-downs, tax resistance, and so on. These methods can be very effective, when employed broadly and strategically. When people work inefficiently, refuse to ride a bus, stop flying flags and singing patriotic songs, or simply stop going to work or school, they are not doing anything violent. It is not violent to take a knee at a football game while the national anthem is playing (to cite one controversial recent example). Nor is it violent to call in sick rather than go to work. Active nonviolent protest is more assertive, involving mass demonstrations, picket lines, and other public and symbolic activities. Un-violent noncooperation is less assertive. But it can also be powerful: there is power in simply doing nothing, when, by doing nothing, we refuse to play along with the status quo, and when in extreme situations we refuse to cooperate with an unjust government or occupying force.

The heroes of nonviolence take a step beyond merely refusing to cooperate. They engage in active nonviolence and in some cases civil disobedience. A step beyond noncooperation takes us to active public protest: marching in demonstrations and picket lines, writing editorials and making public speeches, and so on. A step beyond that occurs when protesters put their bodies on the line in confronting violent opposition, including in some cases the police. Finally, the last step is to put oneself in opposition to unjust authority by breaking the law and publicly challenging the legitimacy of the law and its authorities. All of this creates a risk of retaliation: nonviolent protesters can be threatened, jailed, beaten, and worse.

Nonviolent activities are usually undertaken in defense of noble ends (although it is possible to imagine that racists and others could also take up the techniques of nonviolence). The heroes of nonviolence are celebrated for actively, yet nonviolently, opposing violence, injustice, and oppression. They utilize techniques of organized and deliberate nonviolent action to effect change. It is this effort at nonviolent political action, oriented toward morally praiseworthy ends, that is the focal point of most discussions of nonviolence. We celebrate Gandhi and King, for example, because they employed creative nonviolent action in pursuit of their social and political goals, which included the end of colonialism, racism, and injustice.

Gandhi and King were also, like all human beings, un-violent most of the time. Gandhi especially emphasized an un-violent and simple way of living. But the quotidian world of un-violent simplicity is less glamorous than strikes, marches, boycotts, and public fasts. Nonetheless, there is a continuum in these concepts and terms: nonviolent direct action is related to the un-violence of noncooperation and simple living; and all of this has a further relation to anti-violence movements and even to the counter-violence of peacekeeping forces.

Nonviolence as Root or as Flower?

Given this terminological complexity, it is easy to understand that there are ambiguities in the theory and practice of nonviolence. There are, in general, two ways of conceiving the field or domain of nonviolence. On the one hand, it may be that nonviolence is something that evolves out of violence, representing a higher stage of development that begins with violence and moves beyond it. In this sense, nonviolence may be understood as a flower that develops out of a root of violence. On the other hand, it may be that nonviolence is its own way of thinking and acting: a root or ground of its own, a more primordial or natural background condition from which violence emerges as a disease or defect. In this sense, nonviolence would be the more fundamental category, with violence appearing as a kind of parasite or cancerous growth. Let's call these two ways of thinking the negative and positive views of nonviolence and consider them each in turn.

1.   **Negative Nonviolence.** The negative formulation is contained in the negation of violence seen in the word "nonviolence". This negative formulation points toward a developmental interpretation of nonviolence, seeing it as a flower evolving out of the background of violence. This is nonviolence as the renunciation of violence. There is evidence that Gandhi viewed nonviolence or ahimsa in this way, at least some of the time. One

consideration here has to do with psychological and spiritual development. Young people may be caught up in violence; but there is a sense that we ought to develop beyond that. In a letter to his son, Ramdas, in 1918, the elder Gandhi wrote that a young man must first learn to defend himself; ahimsa comes later. From this perspective, nonviolence is understood as a moral or spiritual development that corrects or refines violence —and that ultimately leads to the refusal to exercise the basic capacity for violence. One way of conceiving this is to focus on the difference between what we have the power to do and what we have the right to do. Nonviolence begins from having the power to use violence —from having the power to destroy. But renunciatory nonviolence maintains that even if we have that power, we ought not use it. Perhaps this is understood as a saintly or supererogatory idea: a higher level of moral and spiritual development involves the renunciation of violence. Or perhaps this is a more general claim which holds that we do not generally have the right to use violence. At any rate, the defenders of nonviolence will argue that a refusal to act violently refines and improves the way that power is deployed. Nonetheless, for nonviolence to arrive as the flower of a higher kind of moral or spiritual development, there must be the original capacity to act violently. This point is important for Gandhi, who does not see nonviolence as mere acquiescence in a condition of powerlessness.

[margin note: not the main goal]

The critics of nonviolence will often complain that it is a weak and cowardly way of giving in to oppressors who are more powerful than you. The critics may also argue that violence is an important tool for demonstrating self-respect and for gaining respect from others. For example, imagine an abused wife who suffers domestic violence at the hand of her domineering and oppressive husband. Some will say not only that an abused wife would be justified in using violence against her abusive husband but also that she would gain a sense of self-respect in finally asserting herself against her oppressor. A similar argument could be made with regard to the violence and oppression suffered by minority communities and those suffering under slavery, colonialism, and political oppression. When the slave rises up and violently resists his master, there is a gain in power and self-respect. Frederick Douglass provides a memorable example in recounting his violent resistance to Mr. Covey, the slave-master, which led him from the "tomb of slavery" to the "heaven of freedom".

Gandhi acknowledged this need for power and self-respect. He made a similar point with regard to the need for India to become a state capable of defending itself. But after making this claim, he explains that once India establishes its power, it ought to move beyond the need to use that power and develop toward nonviolence. The renunciation of violence only comes after the capacity for violence has been demonstrated. He expected India to build its capacity to make war and then renounce it. He said, "A nation that is unfit to fight cannot from experience prove the virtue of not fighting. I do not infer from this that India must fight. But I do say that India must know how to fight. Ahimsa is the eradication of the desire to injure or to kill". What I am calling "negative nonviolence" is the eradication of the desire to do violence. This assumes that prior to nonviolence the desire to kill/harm and the capacity to kill/harm actually exist. This is the sense in which nonviolence is the flower that evolves out of the root of violence.

2. Positive Nonviolence. A different account of nonviolence focuses on nonviolence as the root or background condition of genuine, life-affirming, and constructive power. From this perspective nonviolence is simply what healthy people and societies do: they support life, build relationships, and create meaningful ways of living. Augustine recognized this in *The City of God*. He said that savage animals and human beings naturally seek to live in harmony and peace, suggesting that all living beings by nature love peace. On this view, violence is something that disrupts the normal or natural order of things. This affirmative sense of nonviolence can be found in Gandhi. Martin Luther King Jr. also makes this point clear in his discussion of the affirmative power of love. Love, from this perspective, is the creative and upbuilding force of the universe. We might say in a theological fashion that love is the ground of being, the creative force of the universe, or the power that gives us to be. The idea that peace and love are the background condition of reality is shared by a number of other advocates of nonviolence. Thomas Merton, the Christian mystic, said, "it is to my way of thinking more natural, more in accord with the nature of man, to be non-violent". In a different text, Merton speaks of the wisdom discovered in silence and solitude which points toward "the central unity of Love". All words, Merton says, "say one thing only: that all is Love". This means that violence and hate are deformations of that more fundamental reality —as a cancerous outgrowth or disease coming from a healthy root. Hateful words and violent acts are anomalies and deformations of the original uniting power of love.

We have wandered into the weeds of theology, mysticism, and questions about fundamental reality. Much more could be said. Nonviolence may be a flower or the root. But in general, the point is that nonviolence is best understood in positive terms as creative and strategic use of constructive force —and not as passive withdrawal from life. Nonviolence covers a wide range of actions and behaviors. And when we connect nonviolence with the un-violence of ordinary life, it is easy to see that the domain of nonviolence is much larger than the domain of violence. But, as we shall also see later in this chapter, violence tends to attract our attention —out of proportion to its actual power and extent. This helps explain why nonviolence is often overlooked and taken for granted despite its ubiquity.

Pacifism and Peace

Pacifists are advocates of nonviolence. But some advocates of nonviolence have been reluctant to affirm pacifism. The term pacifism is a fairly recent coinage: it has been traced to the work of Émile Arnaud, who first used the term at the beginning of the twentieth century in the context of a specifically anti-war argument. But Gandhi and King tended to avoid the term. One problem is that "pacifism" sounds like "passive-ism", which makes it seem like compliant, non-resistant, acquiescence to the status quo. Pacifism is also sometimes linked to an other-worldly religious absolutism. And sometimes pacifism is narrowly understood as a rejection of international war. Furthermore, since "peace" (Latin: *pax*) is the root of pacifism, it may seem to imply that peace is the only good that matters. But pacifists usually focus on a comprehensive vision of peace that includes justice and truth. A situation that combines justice with peace might be called "positive peace". On the other hand, a situation in which there is injustice but no overt or direct violence might be considered as "negative peace". Very few pacifists would be willing to exchange justice for peace. Most pacifists have something more comprehensive and positive in mind.

Advocates of nonviolence may have a vision of the good life that is similar to the vision of positive peace. But nonviolence can also be understood merely as a method or strategy of social and political action. Some nonviolent activists will resist employing the label of pacifism because they believe that states have a right to defend themselves with military force. At issue here is a general question about whether violence in its various forms can be justified. Philosophers distinguish, for example, between absolute pacifism and conditional pacifism, as well as between anti-war pacifism, vocational pacifism, and personal pacifism. The conceptual field here is complex and convoluted. Some philosophers have tried to clarify things by introducing new terms. Robert Holmes introduced the term "nonviolentism" to describe a commitment to nonviolence that can be distinguished from pacifism. Holmes and others have also attempted to distinguish between "pacifism" (as an active commitment to positive peace) and "pacific-ism" (as a narrowly focused anti-war position). These distinctions have not caught on among activists and the general public. This terminology is a philosophical convention. Labels are not a primary concern for activists who engage in nonviolence. And such distinctions become slippery in the real world.

Nonviolence as the Constructive Force of Love, Truth, and Justice

Violence can be defined as *the deliberate use of destructive force*. A definition of nonviolence might simply negate that definition: nonviolence is whatever is not deliberately destructive. But this does not mean that nonviolence is non-deliberate destructiveness. Negligent destruction should be remedied and avoided. The heart of nonviolence is aimed at the opposite of destructive force. It is the destruction that matters most —especially when combined with lack of consent, and those violations of autonomy that we call harm or injury. The advocate of nonviolence claims that it is wrong to injure, wrong to harm, and wrong to deliberately use destructive force against someone in an effort to hurt them. Proponents of nonviolence claim that violence is wrong because it is harmful and injurious.

So far, so good. But this still leaves us with a negative formulation of nonviolence as "non-destructive force". But let's push deeper and consider the opposite of destructive force. Destruction has a clear antonym: construction. And here we begin to see the positive values advocated by nonviolence. The proponents of nonviolence want to change the world in constructive ways. So here we discover a useful definition of nonviolence as *the strategic use of constructive force*.

There are many examples of constructive force. Three important concepts have been emphasized by advocates of nonviolence: love, truth, and justice. These three concepts are positive and constructive ideas. To define nonviolence in positive terms we might say that nonviolence develops the power of love, truth, and justice. To act nonviolently is to act lovingly, truthfully, and justly. We might further say that peace is a condition in which love, truth, and justice are actualized. Let's consider each of these values briefly in turn.

A. **Nonviolence is loving.** Love is a broad and complicated concept that includes: romantic or erotic love (what the Greeks called *eros*), the love that exists between friends (what the Greeks called *philia*), love of ideas, love of country, love of wisdom (which is a literal translation of the Greek term *philosophia*), and the love of God and impartial or ethical love (what theologians call *agapē*). In all of these examples, love is something positive, uplifting, and powerful. Love build things. It helps us create and participate in something larger than ourselves. Love is not weak or apathetic. Love inspires and energizes. It gives us strength, vigor, and endurance. And while love is sometimes viewed as a "soft" thing, its softness contains an inner core of firmness and forcefulness —not hardness or coldness, but rather assertive loyalty, affirmative fidelity, and hopeful steadfastness. The opposite of love is hate. Hate is also powerful. But rather than building us up, hate tears down. Hate can energize and give strength. But the strength and power of hate is cold, hard, mean, and vengeful.

Hate is connected to violence, as the goal of hate is to harm, injure, and destroy. But love is central to nonviolence, since its goal is to nurture, build, and create. And in fact, love has long been celebrated as the key to nonviolence. Ancient roots include the Old Testament's commandment to love your neighbor as yourself, which was extended by Jesus in the Sermon on the Mount to require that we also "love our enemies". Martin Luther King Jr. explained this in his "Pilgrimage to Nonviolence" where he said, "The nonviolent resister not only refuses to shoot his opponent but he also refuses to hate him. At the center of nonviolence stands the principle of love". King explains that he came to understand this from studying Gandhi, whose movement was based upon the idea of *satyagraha* —a concept that Gandhi understood as both "love force" and "truth force". Gandhi explained his idea of *satyagraha* as "the force which is born of truth and love, or non-violence". Love is, of course, a broad and complex concept. While it can seem to require saintly sacrifice for the other or romantic obsession with the other, there is also an ethical love that is about reciprocity and equality. If love sounds too elevated, we might think rather in terms of solidarity, which is another way of understanding the concept of "brotherly love". One way of understanding brotherly love is to think in terms of responsibility: to love your neighbor is to take some responsibility for their well-being. Solidarity, reciprocity, equality, and responsibility are central concerns for modern, liberal-democratic politics.

B. Nonviolence is truthful. The Gandhian idea of *satyagraha* (which is translated both as "love force" and as "truth force") shows us the connection between love and truth. Love must be based upon the truth of things. A love (or a loyalty, a commitment, or a patriotism) that is based upon lies and untruths is unstable, fleeting, and mythological. And personal, social, and political structures that are based upon falsehoods require violence, threats, and more lies to keep them in place. Like love, truth is also broad, inclusive, and complicated. Truth can be defined as correspondence with objective reality as well as coherence within a web of belief. For something to be true, it must connect to reality. It must also be coherent, make sense, and be meaningful. Nonviolence holds that truth is constructive. While some truthful claims can appear to be mean and destructive (say, truthful insults), in the long run, truth builds up and reconciles. For example, it is truthful to call out racism and sexism —and to say that racism and sexism are based upon falsehoods, stereotypes, and unjustified biases. While it may seem destructive to say that some person or institution is racist or sexist, the goal of speaking truth to power is not destructive. Rather, it is constructively aimed at transforming the world. The goal is to eliminate harmful lies and replace them with truth. By basing itself in reality and in a meaningful worldview, truthful action is stable, enduring, and inspiring. Truth, on this conception, is not static or boring. Rather, truth grows as we create new ideas, new relationships, and new meanings. Falsehood, which is the opposite of truth, can also grow. Lies build upon lies. A whole web of propaganda and untruth can develop. But as in the parable of the emperor's new clothes, eventually a common-sense critic will point out that a web of lies rests upon the thin threads of unreality, nonsense, prejudice, and hateful stereotypes. This, for example, is what Vaclav Havel meant when he talked about "living in truth" as one of the nonviolent ways that totalitarianism is resisted and undermined. Havel said, "If the main pillar of the system is living a lie, then it is not surprising that the fundamental threat to it is living the truth". While totalitarian regimes such as Havel was arguing against pose violent threats to truth and to truth-tellers, liberal-democratic political systems aim to protect truth from violent repression by mandating protections of freedom of speech and freedom of conscience. One way that this ideal has been described is as a free marketplace of ideas. The metaphor of the marketplace provides a nonviolent image of how truth ought to function. Truth does not require violence to maintain itself. Rather, the truth, as Locke and Jefferson both put it, would do well enough if she were simply left alone.

C. **Nonviolence is just.** Lying and falsehood are related to injustice. Havel points out that totalitarian and authoritarian societies create the illusion of justice. Injustice rests upon webs of untruths and structural violence known as racism, sexism, European supremacy, and the like. What these ideologies have in common is that they do not treat people fairly or respect the dignity of persons. Justice is focused on fair treatment and equal respect for human dignity. It is easy to understand why justice requires nonviolence: to deliberately harm or injure someone is to disrespect them and fail to treat them fairly. Justice may sometimes seem to require violence. The traditional idea of retributive justice (sometimes called the law of retaliation or *lex talionis*) says that we can return evil for evil, harm for harm, and so take an eye for an eye, a tooth for a tooth, and a life for a life. Jesus, Socrates, and other proponents of nonviolence have rejected this idea. One of the reasons for rejecting the *lex talionis* is that it conceives justice as equalizing destructive force. But a constructive view of justice offers something different. It wants to build up, repair, restore, and revitalize. Instead of seeking payback for past harms it looks forward and seeks to create a world of respect, dignity, and justice. The nonviolent alternative to retributive justice is called restorative justice. This does not deny the facts of past misdeeds (truth remains an important value). But rather than seeking retribution, restorative justice seeks to reconcile adversaries and construct a new community. One of the great spokespersons for restorative justice, reconciliation, and forgiveness is the Anglican Archbishop Desmond Tutu —who worked to heal South Africa in the aftermath of the racism, violence, and oppression of apartheid. Tutu puts his idea simply, saying that "there is no future without forgiveness". He connects his ideal of restorative justice to the African value of *ubuntu* as well as to the way that Christian tradition links justice with mercy. Tutu explains, "In the spirit of *ubuntu*, the central concern is the healing of breaches, the redressing of imbalances, the restoration of broken relationships, a seeking to rehabilitate both the victim and the perpetrator, who should be given the opportunity to be reintegrated into the community he has injured". This idea of a community that is balanced and integrated is also a central concern of liberal-democratic polities, where the equality of persons is codified in law and guarantees of equal protection under the law are designed to ensure fair treatment and equality.

Nonviolence is Bigger than Violence

If we accept the basic definition of nonviolence as constructive force, then it is easy to see that nonviolence is a broad and inclusive concept. Love, justice, and truth are similarly expansive concepts. Nonviolence aims to build, grow, and nurture. It looks to the future. It is open-hearted and creative. Nonviolence is also persistent and pervasive. Violence, on the other hand, is narrow, stultifying, backward-looking, and episodic.

To understand my point consider the question of the background conditions of human life. Human existence is generated by the act of erotic love. It is nurtured by motherly and fatherly love. It grows and develops through friendship, social relations, and within a larger political reality characterized by "brotherly love". Normally this unfolds without violence. Of course the question of what counts as "normal" is a normative question that asks us to consider values, purposes, and a background theory of human nature. Some have described the state of nature as a state of war (Thomas Hobbes, for example). But from the vantage point of the nonviolent tradition, war is an aberration and outbreaks of violence are exceptions that occur against a backdrop of nonviolent social life. There are deep questions here, both about empirical reality (whether social life really is best described as nonviolent) and about human purposes and optimal experience (whether violence and war provide us with peak experience or whether love, peace, and truth provide that). There are disagreements about all of this. But the nonviolent tradition insists that social life is mostly nonviolent (in empirical terms) and that the best experiences and relationships (in normative terms) occur in nonviolent activity.

Consider war, for example, as the largest and most egregious case of violence. While some wars last for quite a long time, wars erupt out of a background condition of peace; and wars end with a return to peace. Now those who celebrate violence and war look forward to war as an opportunity to test their virtue and their weapons. There is no denying that, as Chris Hedges put it, "war is a force that gives us meaning". But the nonviolent tradition does not celebrate the goods of war, holding that there are better ways to find meaning and develop virtue. It might be that war can be justified as a last resort, in response to aggression (and limited in other ways by what is called "the just war theory"). But the goal of the just war theory is not to wage continual war. As Augustine, one of the founding thinkers in the just war tradition, put it in a passage quoted with approval by Thomas Aquinas, "We do not seek peace in order to be at war, but we go to war that we may have peace". Aristotle said something similar, that we "make war in order to bring about peace". Rather than celebrating war, the just war theory wants to minimize warfare and would prefer nonviolent conflict resolution rather than war. It is those strategies and techniques of nonviolent conflict resolution that make up the heart of nonviolence.

There are many strategies of nonviolent conflict resolution. In fact, these are the techniques of ordinary social life and democratic politics. Most of the time in most of our lives, we engage in nonviolent activity, including nonviolent conflict resolution. And here we must emphasize that nonviolence does not presume that there will be no conflict or discord. A bland utopian peace theory might seek a world in which there is no conflict. But social life involves conflict. Conflict generates discovery and change. The nonviolent tradition is not opposed to conflict. Rather, it is opposed to violent conflict. And indeed, when thinking about the strategies of nonviolent conflict resolution, it is easy to see that these strategies are wide-ranging and creative. Violence is narrower. In its most brutal form, violence simply eliminates conflict by destroying the other who creates the conflict. Short of outright destruction, violence silences, confines, and restricts opposition and conflict —through threats, prisons, gulags, and social oppression. Nonviolence is less restrictive. Where violence seeks to resolve conflict by stifling freedom and constraining the action of enemies and opponents, nonviolence is more permissive. Rather than eliminating a foe, nonviolence wants to find ways to work with the other and change conditions so that there can be growth, development, and mutual benefit.

More will need to be said about how this happens (and the limits to nonviolent conflict resolution). But let's look for a further clue about the "bigness" of nonviolence in a passage from Plato who said, "it is peace in which each of us should spend most of his life and spend it best". Plato suggests here that the goods of nonviolence are more fully human, more comprehensive, and more important than violence or war. It is nonviolence that allows us to create art, to discover love, and to do science. Nonviolence opens

*while violence can happen,
love is what grows and is the
reason for nonviolence*

the space of education, play, love, and conversation. Family relationships and friendships are built on nonviolence; or they ought to be, unless disrupted by domestic violence and abuse. Work relationships and social networks are built on nonviolence; or they ought to be unless disrupted by workplace harassment and anti-social behavior. And political relationships and the lives of citizens under the rule of law are basically nonviolent, except for those outbursts of violence that we call crime.

To say that nonviolence is bigger than violence is to point out that the normal, natural, and prevailing conditions of human life are nonviolent. To say that nonviolence is better is to say that humans flourish under conditions of nonviolence.

What is Violence?

All of these descriptions of the power of nonviolence rest upon a contrast with violence. But violence is a complex and difficult concept to pin down. On the one hand, violence has to do with the vigor or vehemence of an action. On the other hand, violence has to do with harm and violation. I have defined violence in other work as *the deliberate use of destructive force*. A related definition has been proposed by Michael Nagler, following the work of Johan Galtung: violence is *avoidable insult to human needs*. The Nagler/Galtung definition is intended to allow us to include what is often called "structural violence", which is violence that occurs because of systematic and institutional structures —such as racism, poverty, and so on. But notice that if we use the term violence to describe these structural issues, then violence is removed from the notion of vehemence or vigor: poverty lingers and kills slowly. Poverty is not like a knife thrust, a gunshot, or a blow. My definition —*deliberate use of destructive force*— is not so obviously inclusive. But I think it better reflects the sense of our ordinary usage of the word violence, which is not about avoidable injuries but rather about deliberate harm that involves some kind of immediacy and agency. If we want to use the term violence to talk about structural issues and what we might call "slow violence", we should admit that this is an extension of what is ordinarily meant by the term violence —which is typically episodic, quick, and vehement. The idea of "slow violence" has been explained, for example, by Rob Nixon. He writes, "by slow violence I mean a violence that occurs gradually and out of sight, a violence of delayed destruction that is dispersed across time and space... Violence is customarily conceived as an event or action that is immediate in time, explosive and spectacular in space, and as erupting into instant sensational visibility".

Nixon's definition of slow violence is derivative of a more original sense of violence as something explosive, immediate, visible, sensational, and spectacular. Structural violence is not sensational or spectacular: in a sense it is <u>invisible</u>. Invisible, slow, and structural violence are harmful and deserve serious consideration. But to focus on this kind of violence makes it difficult to understand *nonviolence*. It is not that nonviolence is visible, fast, or episodic (as it would be if nonviolence were understood in opposition to slow/structural violence). Indeed, nonviolence is often slower, less visible, and more sustained than the typical outburst of episodic violence. Nonviolence is often aimed at structural change and is not merely a quick outburst of energy. Indeed, it might be that one sense of the term nonviolence has to do with this slow and sustained effort. The strategies of non-cooperation, demonstrations, marches, boycotts and so on require sustained effort that is slow and steady. This does not mean that such strategies cannot be active, energetic and vehement. Rather, the point is that nonviolent strategies are usually not merely episodic outbursts of energy.

Let's consider further ways that the definition of violence as the deliberate use of destructive force allows us to focus our thinking about nonviolence. First, since this definition of violence focuses on the *deliberate* use of destructive force, it rules out accidental destruction. A husband could move his hand in such a way that his wife's tooth is knocked out. We call this a punch when this movement is deliberate —and typically understand it as violent— in this case, we call this "domestic violence". But if, while dancing, a husband extends his hand and hits his wife in the mouth, this is not really a punch. In fact, it is even problematic to say that such an action amounts to "hitting" the other person. Hitting seems to involve intention. Perhaps we ought to call this accidental contact. At any rate, we would not say that the accidental contact in dance class was violent —in the sense of a deliberate action.

With this in mind, our definition of violence also rules out storms and earthquakes. A hurricane can be quite destructive. But that destruction is not deliberately caused. When we use "violence" in this way to describe non-deliberate occurrences, this is a metaphorical extension of the word that focuses on the vigor, power, or vehemence of something. Notice also that by including the idea of deliberate action, it is possible to affix blame and talk about responsibility. Deliberateness opens the door to moral judgement. It is wrong of a husband to punch his wife. But the accidental contact of dance class is not morally wrong: this was unintentional, the husband did not mean for it to happen, and the husband is not morally responsible for the deed (although he might be negligent or irresponsible in a different sense).

Now let's consider the second part of our definition, which focuses on *destructive force*. This brings in the issue of vehemence and vigor, as well as a different sort of moral judgment. While force that is strong enough to knock out a tooth is violent, a soft touch of a hand on the lips of another person is not violent. One of the things in question here is the power or forcefulness of the action. Another question is about the result —whether it is destructive or not. Consider another case: where a tooth is removed by a dentist. We could imagine an evil dentist violently removing a tooth (say if the dentist kidnaps you and pulls the tooth against your wishes). But dentistry is not violent if you consent to have the tooth pulled and if you (and the dentist) believe that removal of the tooth is good for you. The issue of consent, as well as benefit or harm, must be emphasized. Violence, understood as a kind of violation, occurs when force is not consented to and when that force is destructive or harmful. In this sense, violence is a kind of injury damage, or offence —something done against our will, which violates our autonomy or sense of self and which harms us.

The issues of consent and benefit show us a connection with democratic social and political theory. The democratic theory of government says that governmental authority rests upon the consent of the governed and that states are set up to provide for our common welfare. This can be described in terms of a nonviolently agreed upon social contract. And while governments are said to possess a monopoly on the use of violence in a given geographic area, the basic idea of the social contract is that governmental power should not be based upon violence, threats of violence, or physical coercion but rather upon the freely given consent of those who are subject to the power of the government. As Ackerman and DuVall put it, "real power derives from the consent of those it would control, not from the threat of violence against them". Violence and coercion can, of course, produce concrete political power. The effects of violence are obvious: those who are threatened by violence will adjust their behavior accordingly. But the coercive power of violence deals primarily with bodies and not with the rational thought processes of human persons (i.e., the mind or spirit), even though there is a kind of primitive animalistic rationality involved in threatening violence and avoiding it. In a democratic polity, it is not fear, coercion, and violence that ought to move us but, rather, a shared belief in the legitimacy of governmental authority based upon our belief that the government is here to defend our rights and benefit us. To connect this with our previous discussion we might say that the state is like the dentist: we voluntarily submit to the state's coercive power because we believe it is of benefit to us.

A critique could be mounted of all of this. Anarchists have often pointed out that in reality states are founded on violence and that their power is kept in place by violence or the threat of violence, which is not justifiable and not beneficial. We will consider anarchism again in the last chapter. But the ideal of democratic theory is of a state whose power is not harmful or exploitative: the democratic state is supposed to be founded on consent and not upon violence or the threat of violence.

A further critique would ask about the coercive power of nonviolence. When people engage in boycotts or strikes or campaigns of civil disobedience, some coercion is involved. The boycotters and strikers expect their efforts to have some impact. They are attempting to manipulate their opponent's behavior and force a change. Perhaps nonviolence is not so different from violence, after all. Defenders of nonviolence will insist that nonviolence stops short of causing physical harm. But boycotts can in fact harm people, causing what might be called "collateral damage". Indeed, it is often innocent people who are harmed most by boycotts. In domestic boycotts of corporations, the CEO's and stockholders are less likely to experience significant harms than the hourly workers. In the international arena, rich elites rarely suffer as much under boycotts as the working class and the poor.

We might have to admit that there is actually a continuum here without a precise line distinguishing nonviolence from violence. Property damage, vandalism, and sabotage lie somewhere in the middle of this continuum. On the one hand, it is obviously a violent act to shoot a rocket into a populated city, as has happened, for example in the conflict between Palestinians and Israelis. But it is not clearly violent to paint anti-Israeli graffiti on the border wall or to sabotage it, say by launching an arson balloon or flaming kite at the wall, as has also happened. There will be differing judgments about such cases. But the fact that there is a continuum does not mean that it is not possible to distinguish between obvious cases that involve clear differences.

In the 1970's Barbara Deming offered a theory of nonviolent coercion in response to these kinds of conceptual problems. She claimed that it was possible to employ substantial coercive force, while remaining nonviolent. Central to her theory is the idea that one can exert physical force nonviolently so long as you avoid injuring the other. To get in the way of business, say by blockading a building or stopping traffic, is to engage in physical force. But the goal is not to *injure* the opponent so much as to *frustrate* him. Rather, in Deming's account, "it is quite possible to frustrate another's action without doing him injury". Deming admits that those who are inconvenienced may "feel" that they have been injured. But this is not true she says —especially if those whose interests are frustrated are responsible for injustice and violence. It may frustrate a perpetrator of violence to resist that violence; but interfering with or preventing violence is not itself violent, nor is interfering with or resisting injustice itself unjust. One can see here that there is also a continuum connecting nonviolence with violence employed in self-defense or in defense of others. While many principled proponents of nonviolence (i.e., absolute pacifists) are reluctant to admit the possibility of violence employed in self-defense, such acts can be described as another way of frustrating the purveyor of violence. The question of self-defense opens a number of complicated questions. But the point of considering the possibility of justifying violence in self-defense is not to celebrate violence and thus somehow defeat pacifism. Rather the goal here is to show that there is a continuum that includes nonviolent coercion and active resistance to violence along with the possibility in extreme emergencies of violence employed in self-defense.

And in fact the problem of violence employed in self-defense is the problem of violence in general: it assumes that by killing someone or besting them in a physical struggle, we have completed our work. But nonviolence usually seeks something more than that: not just to destroy or defeat the enemy but to build something better. The goal of nonviolent coercion and strategies of nonviolent noncooperation and interference is not merely coercion but also persuasion and conversion. This then shows us an important difference between violence and nonviolence. Violence is content with coercive power. In a war, the goal is basically to kill the enemy and force them to submit. But in a nonviolent struggle, the submission of the enemy, if we want to call it that, usually ought to lead to something further: justice, reconciliation, and growth —perhaps even the development of what King called "the beloved community".

Now let's push a bit deeper in terms of thinking about *destructive force* and the moral judgment involved. To say that something is destructive appears to make a negative judgment. Normally destruction has a negative connotation. When we say that war is destructive we know what that means, just as it makes sense to say that an abusive husband uses destructive force against his wife. However, sometimes destruction is part of construction. And in other cases, it appears that destruction is justifiable and not negative. Dangerous old buildings must be torn down in order to build safe new ones. Weeds must be destroyed in order to grow food crops. And decaying teeth must be destroyed in order to promote good dental health. It turns out that the idea of destructive force is morally complicated. Does it even make sense to say that weeds must be *destroyed*, for example? We normally say that weeds are plowed under, plucked, cut, cleared, or removed. Of course, from the vantage point of the weed, this is certainly destructive. This may lead us to think that, in a sense, violence is in the eye of the beholder: the gardener does not think he is being violent, while the weed may not agree. Indeed, one person's weed may be another person's flower.

This example is a bit silly. But consider how the question of perspective is found in considerations of abortion, euthanasia, and treatment of animals. Some think that abortion is violent since it destroys a fetus; but defenders of women's right to choose will disagree with such a description. Euthanasia —say in the case of pulling the plug and allowing a braindead person to die— may seem to destroy a human life;

but perhaps a braindead person is already gone and not harmed or destroyed in the process. Vegetarians see eating meat as destructive and violent; but meat-eaters do not. And so it goes. The question of what counts as violence and as destruction opens on to a variety of other considerations, including who or what counts in terms of moral status (who is "a moral patient", as philosophers put it) and whether there is a universal, objective standard that can help us evaluate these kinds of cases.

But let's set aside these deep ethical questions and return to the world of ordinary commonsense. From a commonsense point of view, we don't normally think that we need any special justification for removing a weed. But we may need special justification for tearing down an old building (say, for example, if it is a historical monument). And certainly, we need some justification for using the destructive force of war. If it turns out that some kinds of destructive force may be justified, we may think that this means that such justified destructive force is thus not *violent*. But it may be better to say that while violence is usually presumed to be wrong, there may be some cases in which violence can be justified. Absolute pacifists reject that idea. But some advocates of nonviolence might accept that violence can be justified, while nonetheless continuing to maintain that these cases are rare and that nonviolence remains as a preferred and superior means of changing the world.

Spectacular Violence and Atmospheric Violence

The power of nonviolence is often overlooked, which makes it seem that nonviolence is weak and ineffective. One reason for this is that violence attracts our attention. Spectacular acts of violence stand out against the background of ordinary life which is, in fact, primarily nonviolent (or un-violent to use a term employed above). We can define "spectacular violence" as an act of violence that attracts our attention. Spectacular violence is something we notice, just as we notice the smoke from a fire billowing into the clear air. But violence can also be diffuse and spread invisibly throughout the atmosphere. This diffuse form of violence has been called variously "structural violence", "institutional violence", "systematic violence", and "cultural violence", following Johan Galtung's work. Andrew Fitz-Gibbon has more recently employed a distinction between primary, secondary, and tertiary forms of violence, in a way that focuses on physical harm, psychological harm, and social/cultural harm. These are useful concepts and distinctions. But as mentioned above, my definition of violence as deliberate use of destructive force does not immediately bring to mind structural and cultural violence —since the structures, systems, and institutions that cause "structural violence" do not involve any single person's deliberate choices. And there remain questions about these concepts. Johan

Galtung coined the terms "structural violence" and "cultural violence"; but Kenneth Boulding suggested that this is merely a metaphor. But metaphors are useful. In using the term "violence" to describe social systems that end up hurting people, our imagination is stirred: we begin to see that there is something to notice here. This can also create confusion, however, since we are not sure who the perpetrators of such violence are, what their intentions might be, or what exactly we could do to alleviate or prevent such harms. Nonetheless, the concepts of structural and institutional violence have become firmly established in the theory and practice of nonviolence and peace theory. I suggest, however, that we might employ another metaphor as well: "atmospheric violence". This concept can be found in a hint in Frantz Fanon's work. Fanon writes that under colonialism the atmosphere of violence reeks of "the smell of gunpowder" and violence "ripples under the skin". With cultural violence and structural violence, we smell it more than we see it. Atmospheric violence contaminates the atmosphere and changes our behavior, while also priming the conditions that can lead to direct and overt violence.

As noted, we are playing with metaphorical language here. So let's make it more concrete. Spectacular acts of violence are moments that disrupt an un-violent background. A pleasant social event unfolds without violence; and then a fight breaks out. Those who are gathered together will direct their attention to the violence: they will notice it. The disruptive act of violence will be remembered, while the un-violent background will be mostly forgotten. This is also the way that domestic violence, terrorist attacks, and war occur. These acts of violence erupt out of a nonviolent background. But because they are spectacular and attention-grabbing, we notice and remember them. Atmospheric violence is not noticed in this way. Indeed, it may not be visible at all, until a social scientist starts measuring things with specialized instruments —such as incarceration rates, suicide rates, poverty rates, wealth, health, income, and so on.

This phenomenology of spectacular violence (the account of why we notice and remember it) helps to explain why spectacles of violence are the focus of history, journalism, and art. Historians tend to focus on wars, assassinations, and revolutions because they stand out against the background of daily life. Few historians bother to write a history about the quotidian world of un-violent interaction. Indeed, the discipline of history in the Western world traces itself back to Thucydides who gave us the first real example of historical writing in his history of the Peloponnesian War. Of course, Thucydides is not the first to write about war. Before Thucydides, Homer's epic poetry celebrated the violence of the Trojan War. And the Bible's pages are filled with violence and war: from Cain slaying Abel, to Joshua's triumphant slaughter in the Holy Land, and up to the final battle at

Armageddon. There is something in the very idea of telling a story that seems to dwell on spectacular violence. Violence is what happens: violence is an event appearing against an un-violent background. Nonviolence does not typically happen as an event —it is slow and cumulative. Instead nonviolence is part of the background normalcy against which or out of which the event of violence erupts. When a day or a year or a life passes by in peace, it may seem that there is not much to tell: narrative seems to seek out violence, as the proper subject matter of story-telling. This explains why journalists focus on crime and war, as well as why movies and television shows tend to show war, terrorism, murder, and fighting. No one reads a newspaper to learn that lots of un-violent things happened again today, as usual: that families woke up and ate breakfast, that kids learned in schools, that scientists discovered things, that artists created works of art, and that lovers made love. The headlines are reserved for war, crime, and violence. They are also places where spectacular nonviolence is noted, as when mass demonstrations, boycotts, or strikes occur. But again, spectacular violence often overshadows even obvious and overt acts of nonviolence. If looting or fighting occurs at a demonstration or during a strike, those episodes of violence will attract our attention and divert us. That's why a few violent protesters can derail a nonviolent protest and undermine its efforts.

Atmospheric violence —structural and cultural violence— is different: it does not attract our attention. Structural violence is woven into the institutions and conditions of life: it involves harm, injustice, inequality, and oppression that are part of the social circumstance, as in an apartheid regime. Cultural violence is more focused on the pervasive nature of violent cultural imagery, including the way that the violence we see in culture tends to legitimize actual violence. Galtung suggests that what he calls "personal" violence (which is similar to what I am here calling "spectacular violence") is more manifest to us than cultural or structural violence, which are woven into the background conditions.

With regard to structural and cultural violence, it appears that there is tranquility. But the air is polluted. As Fanon explained with reference to colonialism and anti-colonial violence, under the oppressive conditions of colonialism, violence is everywhere. The colonial oppressor lives upon a network of violence; and the colonized person also lives within this network. There may be the appearance of stability and peace in this system. But the atmosphere is permeated with violence. And a spark can ignite the whole thing. It is easy to see how this occurs in the case of structural violence, when a whole social system is based upon violence. Perhaps it is less obvious with regard to cultural images of violence. But in both cases there is a tendency to normalize violence, making it seem that the world is a violent place in need of violent remedies.

The advocates of nonviolence disagree about this description of the world. They tend to argue that violence is not normal; they hold that violence is not the proper remedy for violence. But atmospheric violence can make it seem as though the proponents of nonviolence are naïve, utopian, and out of touch with reality. For those immersed in the atmosphere of violence, it seems that reality in general —and human nature in particular— is basically violent. And, as Fanon has argued, there is a kind of self-assertion and identity formation that occur when the subjects of violence (the colonized) finally take it upon themselves to fight fire with fire. But the advocates of nonviolence argue that this only leaves the atmosphere more polluted. What is needed, from the standpoint of nonviolence, is to find ways to clean up the atmosphere in order to return things to the natural, normal, and healthy condition of nonviolence.

The advocates of nonviolence will claim that those who think that violence is pervasive are mistaken. Either they dwell on the spectacle of violence while ignoring the pervasive background of nonviolence, or they dwell in a contaminated atmosphere, seeing only a world that is polluted and corrupted by cultural and structural violence. And even in the case of atmospheric violence, the point can also be made that structural and cultural violence is noticed as violence because we understand what it would be like to live in a world that was not permeated by violence.

constructive force but has the power to become destructive

An Objection: Ideological Problems

Before concluding this chapter, let's consider whether violence and nonviolence are merely "in the eye of the beholder". As I put it above, one person's weed may be another person's flower. This example points toward the question of ideology. Nonviolence is the creative use of constructive force. But different people will understand different uses of force as either constructive or destructive. Some will say that capitalism, for example, is a system of nonviolent constructive force. Under capitalism, people engage in trade and commerce: rather than stealing from people or enslaving or killing them, we trade with them. But critics of capitalism have often seen it as a destructive power, which manifests structural violence. Following Marx, critics of capitalism have emphasized that capitalism is alienating and destructive, while also claiming that it rests upon the violence of class conflict. From this point of view, it is the violence of the state (either actual or threatened) that keeps the system of private property in place. If a thief steals from you, the police will be permitted to employ violence in order to capture and punish the thief. But in this example, it is the thief who is called "violent", while the police power is simply taken for granted as a means of preventing that kind of criminal violence.

It is not easy to say what counts as destructive or constructive force. Consider as an example the case of a work stoppage or strike. Let's imagine that workers agree to walk out of the job at a factory and put up a picket line. The purpose of the picket line is, in part, to prevent replacement workers from going to work. Now the owner of the factory may view the work stoppage and the picket line as a kind of violence. The owner may say that the strike is a kind of destructive force: it is destroying the owner's business; it is destroying the shareholder's profits; and so on. If picketers prevent replacement workers from entering the factory, is this violence? What if the strikers pejoratively call the replacement workers "scabs"? What if they lock arms and prevent a replacement from entering the factory? What if they use vandalism against the scab or the owner —say, flattening the tires on their cars? And what if the owner calls the police? If the police are used to break the strike —say by pushing back the picket line— is that violence?

This example shows us the general difficulty, which is that the term "violence" can be employed in ideological ways. Parties engaged in conflict will call one another violent, as a way of justifying defensive violence. And the state's "monopoly on violence" (as Max Weber put it) is often not even understood as violence. The dominant culture does not view the criminal justice system as a system of violence. But minority and dissident cultures may in fact suffer direct violence (in the form of arrest, police killings, torture, and so on) and will often claim that there is structural violence woven into that system.

Similar ideological problems arise in thinking about the concepts related to nonviolence discussed above: love, truth, and justice. For example, is love gendered and how is it connected to sex, marital rituals, and so on? With regard to truth, we know that there are deep disputes among religions, between religious people and the non-religious, and among divergent political parties. Justice can also be analyzed from the perspective of ideology, with fundamental disagreements about who counts as a citizen (and even a person), how equality is to be balanced with liberty, and the very source and meaning of the law.

Obviously we cannot solve all of these problems here. A more robust and comprehensive philosophy of nonviolence would work its way through these issues in detail. And, in fact, the most influential proponents of nonviolence have typically understood the need for a more comprehensive account. With Gandhi and King, for example, the theory and practice of nonviolence are connected to religious and political traditions that help to flesh out some of these details. But even these traditions can be subjected to ideological critique, and Gandhi and King have been criticized by feminists and others who point out the ideological limitations of their theory and practice.

For our purposes here, let's conclude by noting that one of the interesting features of nonviolence is that it opens the door toward these critical questions. There is a risk of relativism here. But we must also insist on some objectivity in defining harm, injury, and violence. Without some basic agreement about the wrongness, for example, of police killing unarmed people, we end up in a relativist quagmire. At some point, we must find some consensus and agreement about what it means to speak of "constructive force" and "destructive force".

But, and here is the point, the proponents of nonviolence have typically been willing to engage in a critical project of interpretation and analysis because they tend to think that that sort of analysis is constructive! Said differently, nonviolence tends to involve those kinds of creative and thoughtful analyses that give rise to critical political and philosophical questions. Violence in its most basic form is dumb, animalistic, and brutal. Violence typically involves the push and pull of physical force. Its aim is to shut up and eliminate others. But nonviolence occurs at a different level, appealing to a more human and rational domain. It is more inclusive and dialogical. This is why many of the advocates of nonviolence imply that nonviolence is a higher path, connected to something like wisdom, enlightenment, and moral development. These terms can also be subjected to an ideological analysis. But the advocates of nonviolence tend to understand that. Nonviolence is not just a way of saying no by destroying. Rather, it is an invitation to further creative, constructive activity, including the activity of thinking about nonviolence itself.

Chapter 3

The Who and Whom of Nonviolence. Who practices nonviolence? To whom is nonviolence directed?

Discussions of nonviolence often dwell on exceptional cases of heroic nonviolence, say when a person dedicates their life to a nonviolent movement. Great heroic acts of nonviolence involve self-sacrifice and sometimes martyrdom. These heroic acts are exemplified by individuals such as Gandhi or King. The heroes of nonviolence lead and organize mass movements. Sometimes they are jailed. Sometimes they are killed, as King and Gandhi were. And sometimes they simply disappear, as did the man who stood in front of a tank in Tiananmen Square in 1989. But for every such hero, there are thousands and millions of supporters, marching, chanting, and acting nonviolently among the masses that make up the mass movement. There is a natural tendency to focus on those heroic individuals who exemplify the practice of political nonviolence. Nonviolence is most dramatic and noticeable when it stops a tank or moves the masses. But nonviolence is also pervasive and persistent. As a political force it gains its power from the masses who march anonymously behind the famous leader, from the individuals who go to the polls, from all of those who join in a boycott or act of noncooperation, and from all of the teachers, nurses, scientists, lawyers, clergy, and parents who engage in the constructive project of quietly supporting peace, truth, justice, and love.

Indeed, nonviolence is often quite ordinary. Most of us practice nonviolence most of the time. And what Gandhi called "the constructive program" is ultimately focused on a transformed way of life that avoids violence by creating human connection and fulfilling human needs in positive ways. Nonviolence is the background condition of normal human life. This is true even within racist and oppressive societies. The daily lives of most people —even within racist and oppressive societies— consists in going to work, caring for friends and family, and so on. Admittedly there is something perverse about a society where people behave nonviolently within a circle of privilege, while the social, political, and historical context rests upon violence. Would we want to say that the average citizen of Nazi Germany in the

1930's was living nonviolently when the Nazis were brutalizing the Jews and gearing up for war? Would we want to say that American colonists were living nonviolently in New England towns, when the land had been expropriated from native peoples, when slavery was fueling the economy, and when there was ongoing violence on the borderlands?

were ppl acting like lovalists of just staying quiet

When the nonviolent lives of some people rest upon a bed of violence used against others, this is "structural violence", as discussed in the previous chapter. The problem of structural violence is that the circle of nonviolence in such societies is closed: there is nonviolence within the dominant group, which excludes "the other", those who are liable to receive the negative impact of oppression and violence. The quotidian nonviolence found within structurally violent regimes indicates inconsistency and hypocrisy. It seems wrong for some people to enjoy the nonviolent goods of ordinary life, while others do not: playing, learning, loving, working, and so on. The goods of human life ought to be enjoyed by everyone in conditions of positive peace: we flourish when we engage in nonviolent activities with one another. The critique of structural violence tells us that we should overcome the hypocrisy and inconsistency of structural violence by extending the goods of nonviolent life widely to all human beings —and possibly also to nonhuman beings.

one group is benefitting from the problem

To understand this requires that we delve into what we might call "social ontology". Nonviolence asks us to reconsider social relations. It asks us to consider who gets to enjoy the goods of life and to whom we have obligations of care. The historical proponents of nonviolence focus on interdependence and interconnection. They tend to say things like "all men are brothers" or to use non-gendered language, "all persons are interrelated". We might call this the "domestic analogy" of nonviolence. This idea of a "domestic analogy" has typically been employed in thinking about the justification of war: just war theorists want us to think about national self-defense in terms of an analogy with individual defense (or defense of loved ones within the household). But the advocates of nonviolence have routinely employed a different kind of domestic analogy: asking us to think of the human family as interrelated. Within the human family, nonviolence, solidarity, and love should be the primary values. Nonviolence promotes a way of understanding social life that breaks down the distinction between us and them, self and other —and which offers a criticism of those ways of thinking that create hierarchies and structures of domination. Social hierarchies are often built upon violence, with one class, race, or gender dominating another. Nonviolence wants to build a different social world using, of course, nonviolent means. Nonviolence is not then merely a strategic method or tool for the powerless to employ against the powerful with the goal of attaining power. Nonviolence also contains a transformative social ontology that aims to abolish the hierarchical distinction between the powerful and the powerless, while reconstructing social relations in a way that eliminates hierarchical violence itself. Said differently, nonviolence is compassionate and constructive engagement with the wide world that aims to promote flourishing in a world of equality, fairness, and justice.

2. People raise their hands and shout slogans while carrying voting ballots used in the banned independence referendum during the October 1st, 2017 protests in Barcelona to claim the independence of Catalonia.

In this chapter, we will explore the social standpoint of the call for nonviolence. This extends to the question of whether nonviolence is appropriate for those with political authority: the police, the military, and so on. Nonviolence is often seen as a method for those who lack the power and authority to take charge of their own destiny. But the proponents of nonviolence do not believe that nonviolence is only a concern for the powerless who are struggling against the powerful. Indeed, there is something perverse about demanding that oppressed people behave nonviolently, when the very condition of their oppression is the violence of their oppressors. In its broadest manifestation, the goal of nonviolence is a world in which everyone behaves nonviolently, including the powerful.

The Global Tradition of Nonviolence

We briefly discussed the history of nonviolence in Chapter 1. We return to this now, with a bit more detail in order to show how broad the appeal to nonviolence is. Nonviolence is not merely the dream of a few idealists. Rather, there is a broad global tradition of nonviolence, which weaves together ideas found in many of the world's cultures. This tradition includes key terms taken from multiple traditions: *satyagraha* (Gandhi's idea of "truth-force"), *ahimsa* (the South Asian word for nonviolence), *ubuntu* (the Southern African concept of "humaneness" and interconnection), and *agape* (the Christian idea of disinterested and universal love). Proponents of nonviolence have learned from different traditions and have worked to articulate a vision of nonviolence that is inclusive and comprehensive.

And yet, when it comes to the question of who practices nonviolence, one answer may be that nonviolence is only for a few privileged people, perhaps only for those saintly figures who lead movements and who are willing to sacrifice and even be martyred. This is related to what is sometimes called vocational pacifism or personal pacifism, which only requires nonviolence of those who have taken an explicit vow of nonviolence. We see this, for example, in some religious traditions, where the clergy are committed to nonviolence but ordinary laypeople are not required to take a similar vow. A related idea might be found in medical ethics, where there is a commitment to the principle of doing no harm. On some interpretations, this means that in war, a nurse or doctor may heal the sick but not take up arms. But in general the philosophy of nonviolence is not supposed to be a "vocational" issue in this way. Rather, the proponents of nonviolence tend to think that this is a universal good: that all people should practice nonviolence.

Nonviolence is thus not something special that only a saintly few are capable of. Many of the advocates of nonviolence have been turned into saintly beings in the popular imagination. Consider the accolades and honorific titles given to people such as the Mahatma Gandhi: the term *mahatma* means "great soul" or saint. Martin Luther King Jr. was a Christian pastor who has been revered as a kind of American saint. Desmond Tutu is an archbishop who has been called a "living saint". Pope Francis is a pope who took his name from Saint Francis of Assisi. And the Dalai Lama is held to be a reincarnated holy spirit, an emanation of the Bodhisattva Avalokiteshvara. Despite the mystical holiness associated with these figures, their message is not that we ought to become saints. Rather, there is hope that ordinary people can and should behave nonviolently. Indeed, some of the other advocates of nonviolence we have discussed —Malala Yousafzai, for example— provide an example of the way that ordinary people can embrace and advocate for nonviolence.

The cast of characters we have named here has more in common than the fact that they advocate and practice nonviolence. These folks also reside on the margins of power. Nonviolence is often understood as a tool for the marginalized: for religious minorities, for people of color, or for women. It is true that nonviolence is a powerful tool for marginalized people. But, as mentioned above, nonviolence is not merely a tool for the powerless. It is the powerful, especially, who ought to learn the wisdom of nonviolence.

In the Western tradition, the idea of nonviolence can be traced back to Jesus. Jesus and his movement were outsiders in the Roman and Jewish hierarchy of ancient Judea. This outsider's perspective helps explain the nonviolent heart of Western/ Christian pacifism as found in a couple of key passages taken from Jesus's Sermon on the Mount (Matthew 5-7). Jesus says, for example to "turn the other cheek" and not to return evil for evil. This is based upon a basic ethic of love: love of neighbor and love even of one's enemy.

The Power of Love

Martin Luther King Jr.'s words provide a powerful source of inspiration. King sees nonviolence in connection with the power of love. His hopeful effort aims to transform the heart by developing a shared sense of justice, truth, and love. As a Christian, King understands love as the background condition of reality. King's notion of love is the Christian idea of *agape* —disinterested, ethical love. He says, "In the final analysis, agape means a recognition of the fact that all life is interrelated. All humanity is involved in a single process, and all men are brothers". He said, "To the degree that I harm my brother, no matter what he is doing to me, to that extent I am harming myself... Why is this? Because men are brothers. If you harm me, you harm yourself. King further explains that love is an active power that preserves and creates community. The sense of interrelatedness is crucial for a positive account of nonviolence. King explains:

> Love is the only force capable of transforming an enemy into a friend. We never get rid of an enemy by meeting hate with hate; we get rid of an enemy by getting rid of enmity. By its very nature, hate destroys and tears down; by its very nature, love creates and builds up. Love transforms with redemptive power.

This idea, that we are all interrelated, goes so far as to call upon us to include our enemies in the circle of nonviolent concern. Jesus said that we should love our enemies and pray for those who persecute us (Matthew 5). This means that nonviolence is connected to forgiveness and reconciliation. Now some may think that the command to love your enemies goes too far: enemies may take advantage of love and forgiveness. Prudence and strategy are important here. To love your enemy does not mean that you ought to allow them to oppress you. But the more general point is that there is a call for us to expand the circle of concern: the answer to the question of "nonviolence to whom" may extend to include even our enemies.

The loving and nonviolent ideal of Jesus makes sense, when we consider that Jesus was a powerless rabbi who was an outsider to the halls of power. It makes sense to call for turning the other cheek and loving your enemies, when you do not have an army or the capacity to fight your enemies. But Jesus did not say that only the powerless should be nonviolent. And his strategy was, as Walter Wink has explained in detail, to stand up to the powerful and demand to be treated as an equal. In Wink's interpretation, to turn the other cheek means to stand up to abuse and demand to be recognized as an equal: rather than cowering, you assert your dignity by offering your cheek to your oppressor.

stand up for yourself

Christians interpret the Bible in various ways. Some take the Gospel passages about nonviolence very seriously. We see this in the Anabaptist traditions of Europe, in American Transcendentalist Christianity, and in Tolstoy's reinterpretation of Russian Orthodoxy. These forms of Christianity were often marginalized by the mainstream of Christianity, which tended to downplay nonviolence in favor of crusades, just wars, and inquisitions. Tolstoy, for example, was excommunicated by the Russian Orthodox Church. A significant difficulty confronted by the nonviolent tradition is that nonviolence does not fit well within the prevailing ideology of political, military, and religious power.

Jesus, was of course, executed by the authorities. He asked for forgiveness for his executors from the cross. And the Romans oppressed and martyred Christians for many long years. The Jesus story seems to show that calls for nonviolence will be unheeded by the authorities when articulated from the margins of power. A similar story could be told about Socrates. Socrates was convicted by Athens and sentenced to death. While in prison, Socrates discussed power and authority with a friend named Crito, who urged him to escape. But Socrates said, "we ought neither to requite wrong with wrong nor to do evil to anyone, no matter what he may have done to us". Socrates's idea about not returning evil for evil predates Jesus by several hundred years. But, like Jesus, Socrates was killed.

But —and here is the good news— the models of Jesus and Socrates continued to inspire the world. These Greek and Christian sources gave rise to a 2,000-year long conversation about power, justice, authority, and nonviolence. Some argue that violence can be justified. Others maintain that nonviolence remains the higher path. In other parts of the world, there are parallel discussions. There are traditions of nonviolence in the Islamic world, in China, in South Asia, and in Africa. The world heritage of nonviolence is drawn together in a way by Mohandas K. Gandhi, who exemplifies a kind of cosmopolitan, multicultural, and modern theory and practice of nonviolence. The global history of nonviolence is too large for us to recount here. So let's focus our attention on Gandhi, in order to see how the traditions of nonviolence merge and mingle.

Gandhi resides at the intersection of cultures. He was born in British-ruled India. He went to London to study law. He worked in South Africa, where he first developed his techniques of nonviolent activism, working to defend the rights of the Indian minority in South Africa. In South Africa, he founded his first commune or *ashram* and began a process of transforming the way he and his family lived. While in jail in South Africa, Gandhi studied the works of Henry David Thoreau and Leo Tolstoy. He eventually founded a cooperative farm in South Africa, called Tolstoy Farm, where labor was linked to spiritual development. After successfully working to defend

Indian rights in South Africa, Gandhi returned to India, where he employed a variety of nonviolent tactics —including marches, civil disobedience, and fasting— to tackle issues of social justice and to work for Indian self-rule. In India, Gandhi worked with a coalition of supporters including both Hindus and Muslims. Eventually the British were driven out of India. But ethnic and religious divisions led to bloodshed. India was partitioned. Gandhi was eventually murdered by a Hindu nationalist.

Gandhi wove together influences from a variety of traditions including both South Asian and Western/Christian sources. His idea of *ahimsa* is rooted in the Indian religions and philosophies of Jainism, Hinduism, and Buddhism. But Gandhi also worked with Muslims such as Maulana Azad and Khan Abdul Ghaffar Khan, who inspired an Islamic nonviolent movement that worked in concert with Gandhi. Gandhi's theory and practice went on to influence James Lawson and Martin Luther King Jr. as they used nonviolence to combat racism in the United States. The American example had a tragic conclusion in the assassination of Dr. King; but it was also successful insofar as it led to civil rights legislation and a continued struggle against racism. In the subsequent decades, James Lawson has continued to train people in the tactics and philosophy of nonviolence. A whole network of activist groups and scholarly investigation has developed, which continues to study and implement nonviolence through journals, books, workshops, and academic programs in "peace studies" or "peace and conflict studies". Today there is a developed tradition of nonviolence that includes a refined set of concepts, empirical studies, and training resources. This work has provided an inspiration for successful nonviolent movements across the globe.

Two important points should to be made here in concluding this brief discussion of the tradition of nonviolence. First, nonviolent struggle has proven to be effective. And second, the tradition continues to evolve. The tradition of nonviolence has included those who advocated for a kind of non-resistance that simply acquiesced to power (sometimes called "passive resistance"); but with Gandhi nonviolence becomes active and strategic. As these techniques were honed and further developed, they have become more successful. Empirical studies show how and why nonviolence has worked. This has in turn influenced changing strategies and techniques of nonviolence. These changing techniques depend upon social context, the political situation, and available technologies. In the nineteenth century, Thoreau experimented with tax-resistance as a kind of civil disobedience. In the early part of the twentieth century, Gandhian satyagraha involved marches and symbolic disobedience. Decades later, Lawson, King, and Rosa Parks masterminded boycotts and lunch counter sit-ins. Central Europeans protested Soviet rule by taking to the streets and emphasizing solidarity in civil resistance. In the twenty-first century, the internet and cellular technologies have allowed for mass mobilization, flash mobs, and "occupations" of public spaces. As information spreads and solidarity develops, there are evolving techniques of divestment, boycotts, and so on. While Gandhi and King provide the inspiration for much of this, the tradition of nonviolence is not static. The work continues with new generations of scholars and activists addressing new issues in creative ways. And with the ease of communication provided by the Internet and social media, there is a democratizing tendency in the work of nonviolence, with young people like Malala Yousafzai and Greta Thunberg emerging as inspirational voices in the call for nonviolent social change.

Who and To Whom?

Nonviolence is not merely something that only saints can practice. Rather, it is something we all do most of the time: we employ constructive force with our families, friends, and coworkers every day. And in those mass nonviolent movements that promote social change, it is the ordinary person who matters. The leaders of these movements get most of the attention. But leaders could not succeed without millions of ordinary people who walk out on strike, sit down in protest, march through the streets, and lock arms to demonstrate solidarity.

One substantial problem in thinking about the who and whom of nonviolence is that those who are nonviolent within a narrow circle of others may also allow violence to occur and sometimes even actively engage in violence against others who are not included within their circle of nonviolent concern. This problem lies at the heart of structural violence. Sexist or racist societies, for example, can exhibit a veneer of peace that rests upon a deeper kind of background violence. White racists may exhibit nonviolent brotherhood with other whites, while supporting or actively participating in violence against non-white minorities. The same ambivalence is also found in the middle of war. Brothers-in-arms are nonviolent toward one another, even as they employ violence against the enemy. And a general populace of patriots behaves nonviolently with one another, while harboring ill-will and supporting violence against the enemy.

The advocates of nonviolence are usually quite critical of this kind of ambivalence. They generally want us to extend and expand the circle of nonviolence. It's not enough merely to be nonviolent within a closed circle of friends. There is a universalizing impulse in nonviolence. The ideal is for everyone to practice nonviolence (the who) toward everyone else (the whom).

The advocates of nonviolence maintain that each of us should be nonviolent. And each of us should also feel a sense of responsibility for violence that is committed in our names and with our consent and permission. The advocates of nonviolence tend to be critical both of acting violently and of allowing violence to occur. It is obviously wrong to deliberately employ violence. But it is also wrong to hire another to engage in violence. And it is even wrong to permit violence. But nonviolence is not merely negative: it is also about constructive engagement. Thus the advocates of nonviolence tell us that we ought to be constructively engaged with the world in a variety of ways. Everyone ought to build up and support habits and attitudes of constructive engagement. Each person ought to try to spread love, justice, and truth, as well as equality, fairness, and respect. We will turn to these positive values below. But let's first dig further into the negative prohibition against committing and allowing violence.

It is obviously wrong from the standpoint of nonviolence to instigate a violent attack. But what if one is attacked? Difficult questions arise here that are related to the question of who and whom. Some proponents of nonviolence will say that there is no exception to the prohibition against violence, even in case of attack. This idea is known as absolute pacifism. In response, others will defend the idea that violence can be employed in self-defense. Arguments about defensive violence focus on the questions of who and whom. People who are not under attack may not use violence. But there may be a special exception for those who are under attack (or when you have a special obligation to protect those who are under attack). The justification of using violence in self-defense also contains a specific limitation on whom: the violence of self-defense is supposed to be narrowly targeted at the one who instigated the initial attack. One well-established theory of the justification of using violence in self-defense is known as "the just war theory". This theory stipulates a variety of restrictions about the use of violence in war. Important concerns among these stipulations are the following: violence ought only to be used for defensive purposes; violence ought to be narrowly targeted; the intention behind violence should not be selfish or violent; and there should be opportunities for reconciliation and peace-making.

Proponents of nonviolence will, however, raise critical questions about defensive violence. Some advocates of nonviolence (i.e., absolute pacifists) will say simply say that we have a duty not to engage in violence. But one need not be an absolutist to think that responsible agents ought to avoid using violence whenever possible. A significant concern here is that it is not easy to limit violence once it is engaged: a narrowly focused moral intention can give way to cruelty, brutality, and escalation. In the context of warfare, this problem is laid bare in discussions of war crimes and moral injury. Even "good guys" can end up committing atrocities and violating just war prohibitions. When this happens, soldiers can end up experiencing moral injury, which occurs when soldiers understand that they have been engaged in activities that violate their own conscience and sense of self. Furthermore, advocates of nonviolence argue that everyone deserves to be protected from violence and should have a kind of immunity from violence. The idea of immunity is interesting. This sphere of protection or immunity —the class of beings who should be protected from violence— is defined in various ways. In the context of war this is known as "noncombatant immunity": non-fighters (e.g., civilians) should not be killed and destructive force ought to be narrowly targeted at combatants. One of the difficulties of war, however, is that violence spreads and noncombatants are often killed. In more general terms, the proponents of nonviolence extend the sphere of immunity widely.

Minimizing Violence and Finding Alternatives

To deliberately choose to use destructive force implies a kind of freedom of choice. But if you are being attacked (or if your friends or family are under attack) it may be that freedom of choice is lacking. Those who defend the idea of justified violence used in self-defense (or in defense of another) will often say that "we have no other choice but to use violence" or that "violence is necessary". This implies that defensive violence is not freely chosen or that violence used in self-defense is merely responsive or reactive. From this point of view, the original attack is wrong; but the violence employed in response to the original attack is essentially connected to the wrongness of the original attack. The proponent of defensive violence will say that it is not my fault that I must use violence to defend myself against a violent attack: the responsibility here rests entirely with the one who instigated the attack.

There is much more that could be said about the justification of violence in self-defense. These discussions spill over into discussions of the justification of defensive wars. Absolutizing conclusions are not helpful here and it is likely that even ardent advocates of nonviolence will agree with Gandhi that if there is no other way to avoid violence, some violence may be justifiable. But the point of nonviolence is not to dwell on such exceptional circumstances. Rather, the goal is to seek nonviolent alternatives. Advocates of nonviolence typically try to find ways to minimize and restrict violence. Two ideas are typical: (1) the idea of preventive nonviolence, including nonviolent conflict resolution; and (2) the idea of nonviolent defense or nonviolent self-defense.

With regard to preventive nonviolence and conflict resolution, the idea is that once we are in a situation where an attack occurs, it is often too late. From the standpoint of nonviolence it is better to defuse conflict prior to escalation toward violence. And if escalation is already underway, the goal is to minimize violence and de-escalate. This is complicated, to say the least. But there are various techniques of de-escalation, de-polarization, and nonviolent conflict resolution —in both international relations (in diplomacy and war) and in interpersonal relations (in business, politics, family, and social life). In general, the goal is to move toward something like a "de-escalatory spiral" by working to change perceptions, encouraging dialogue, understanding hierarchies of needs and wants, avoiding polarizing stereotypes, pausing hostilities to create a "cooling off period", and in general working to minimize violence. But if violence is already on the scene, there are also techniques of nonviolent defense. Some Asian martial arts provide methods of self-defense that aim to de-escalate or disable while minimizing violence. At the personal level, there are various techniques of confrontation and avoidance, including screaming, running, and the use of minimal violence such as pepper spray. In war and policing, there have been efforts to develop weapons that are less violent: water cannons, rubber bullets, tear gas, sonic and ultrasonic weapons. The point of these techniques is to find a way to "fight" that minimizes violence and tries to avoid escalating to the level of killing the attacker.

Advocates of nonviolence have developed related techniques of nonviolent intervention including: nonviolent interposition, protective accompaniment, or what is called "third party nonviolent intervention". The basic idea is that violence can be avoided or defused when there are witnesses and others who stand by, accompany and support victims and potential victims of violence. With regard to bullying, for example, bystanders can stop bullying by stepping in or speaking out. Proponents of nonviolence build upon these techniques to argue in favor of non-military national defense, described in various ways as "civilian based defense", "peace brigades", and "peace armies". Gandhi and his followers imagined nonviolent "peace armies" (*shanti sena*) that would provide resistance to oppressive government —and even to an invading army. Gene Sharp has explained how civilian based defense (also called post-military defense or social defense) can be more effective than military defense, even in the face of foreign invasion. We will discuss details in the next chapter. But the methods include non-cooperation, civil resistance, and what Sharp calls "political jiujitsu" that makes it impossible for an oppressive government or invading power to maintain control.

There are many examples of how this idea has been put into action, some more successful than others. In the 1930's, for example, under the leadership of Khan Abdul Ghaffar Khan, a brigade of nonviolent protestors stood up against the British, who massacred them at Kissa Kahani Bazaar. Many died; but eventually the British lost power. More recently, peace workers have travelled to conflict zones —in Latin America and Asia, for example— to provide escorts, witnesses, monitors, and support. In extreme cases, advocates of nonviolence have offered themselves up as voluntary "human shields" in zones of conflict, with varying degrees of success. In the run up to the 2003 invasion of Iraq, dozens of peace advocates voluntarily went to Iraq, acting as human shields. They did not avert the invasion; but they succeeded in drawing critical attention to the war.

The idea of non-cooperation to an invading army had been proposed by Gandhi, who had imagined nonviolent resistance to a possible Japanese invasion of India in the early 1940's. He recognized that this would be brutal and could possibly lead to the extermination of large numbers of nonviolent resisters. But he suggested that if the peace army were disciplined and determined it could be effective, even though he admitted that it was possible that the invader would "exterminate all resisters". This puts the question in stark relief: extermination or submission. Gandhi did not think it would come to this eventuality, holding out the hope that the invading army would grow tired of killing. For critics of nonviolence, this could be seen as a ridiculous and immoral point of view. But the proponent of nonviolence will point out that it is no more ridiculous than the kind of mass slaughter that is taken for granted as a necessary means by proponents of war.

As Sharp and others who have studied empirical and historical details have noted, there are examples of successful nonviolent civil defense. One key to this is training and preparation. Armies and police are well-trained and well-funded. Proponents of civilian-based, nonviolent defense have argued that if people were similarly trained and prepared, they could be more successful. We might also add that it is perverse to demand perfect nonviolence and strategic coherence of the un-trained people who join in a demonstration or mass movement. Successful nonviolent campaigns require systematic coordination, training, and support.

Responsibility and the Expanding Circle of Concern

The issue of third-party involvement is significant for peace work, involving both the news media and the international community. One way of preventing and defusing violence on the international scale is for third parties to get involved both by exposing violence and by bringing negative pressure to bear on those who promote and purvey violence. Often campaigns of social change involve a substantial focus on self-help, with the victims of violence and injustice working on their own behalf to change things. But in some cases, the victims of violence are disempowered and unable to resist violence and promote change without the help of third parties. Thus there is a complex interchange between and among the actors and spectators in nonviolent campaigns. Sometimes the focus of a nonviolent action is on those who are protested against. But sometimes the focus is on a third party, as a kind of appeal for help. Third parties can help by offering sanctuary and support to nonviolent protestors and resisters. Third parties can also put pressure upon the purveyors of nonviolence. The media is involved in these cases in a similarly complex way, reporting upon the travails of the victims, the tactics of the nonviolent resisters, and the strategies that the dominant party employs to resist the resisters. And the question of responsibility is similarly complicated. Are third parties responsible when they ignore violence and look the other way? Is the media responsible when it only reports from the dominant perspective, without investigating the tribulations of the victims of violence?

This question of responsibility leads us back to the question of outsourcing violence and allowing others to perpetrate violence. We mentioned, above, a couple of other cases where violence is wrong: that it is wrong to employ another to engage in violence; and that it may even be wrong to permit violence. The first case seems fairly obvious: if it is wrong for you to do something, then it is also wrong for you to hire someone else to do that thing. Of course, one may raise an objection to vocational pacifism with this in mind: does the priest or medic who rejects violence simply "outsource" violence as a part of the division of labor, asking someone else to do the dirty work, while he keeps his hands clean? This is a difficult question, which deserves further reflection. It is related to the question of whether it is wrong to permit violence. So let's turn to that question now.

If violence in general is wrong, then each of us may have a substantial responsibility to prevent violence from happening. This is generally the idea that we find behind critiques of structural violence. If my well-being depends upon a system that engages in violence, then I am in a sense responsible for this violence. The beneficiaries of apartheid regimes, colonial occupations, and even genocide may not themselves engage in direct violence against "the other". But their benefit comes at the expense of those who suffer under violence. No legitimate ethicist would say that it is OK to hire someone to carry out genocide or a colonizing war on your behalf. The question of whether it is permissible to enjoy the benefits of genocide and colonialism is morally vexing. One problem is that the networks of cause and effect, harm and benefit are often complex and diffuse. Furthermore, those of us who are the beneficiaries of past genocides and colonialism are not directly involved in those past harms. A further problem is that the question of how to make amends for past violence is made more difficult by the question of to whom we would give reparations or apology.

There is also a complicated conceptual distinction between doing and allowing. With regard to structural violence, the question is the extent to which the beneficiaries of structural violence actually do something to cause violence or whether they merely allow it to happen. Even if one is not a beneficiary, there is a remaining question of how much responsibility we have to prevent violence and save others. Our thinking about this will likely depend on a number of issues including: our proximity to those who are suffering, our ability to help, the capacity of suffering people to help themselves, and the kind of threat and harm that these people are suffering under. The philosopher Peter Singer has provided a striking thought experiment to guide our thinking about this. He suggests that if we see a child drowning in a nearby puddle, we have an obligation to save the child —even if we get our shoes muddy. By analogy he says that if people on the other of the globe are dying of easily remedied starvation, we have an obligation to help. If it is in our power to help —and if by helping we do not suffer significant losses or threats of harm— we ought to help.

Now imagine a child is suffering from violence, say his parents are beating him. Do we have an obligation to intervene? Proponents of nonviolence may say we have an obligation to intervene, so long as our intervention is nonviolent. We could do this by offering support for the abused child, by bearing witness to the abuse, or in extreme cases helping the child escape. It is not enough to avoid committing violence; we also may have a positive obligation to prevent violence. A utilitarian such as Singer might agree about this case, although for different reasons (and without stipulating any requirement about avoiding violence when we intervene). This child abuse example is not a case of structural violence —it is about intervening to rescue someone from direct, personal violence. But what about structural violence? Global hunger and starvation can be understood in terms of structural violence. Singer's thought experiment seems to imply that if someone is suffering from structural violence, we have an obligation to help that person. But is suffering under racial injustice similar to drowning in a pond, being beaten by one's parents, or dying of starvation? There is much to think about here. In general, the proponents of nonviolence seem to support the idea that we have extensive obligations to prevent direct violence and to work against structural violence —so long as our efforts remain nonviolent. Others will argue that in working against violence, some kind of violence can be employed, as in the case of using the military in rescue operations known as "humanitarian interventions". Defenders of violent humanitarian interventions will claim that we have a "responsibility to protect" vulnerable people who are being abused and oppressed by their own governments. Proponents of nonviolence may agree that we have a responsibility to protect while disagreeing about the appropriate means to be employed: preferring nonviolent means of protection. With regard to structural violence and its remedies there is a similar discussion. Some revolutionaries call for violence in opposition to structural injustices, apartheid, and oppression; but the advocates of nonviolence call for nonviolent action against these structural injustices.

3. Martin Luther King Jr. with leaders of The March at the White House, Washington, D.C. August 28, 1963.

As we have seen here, there are significant questions about the extent of our responsibility. To whom are we obligated when it comes to protection from violence? Some advocates of nonviolence seem to imply that there is a universal obligation. Martin Luther King Jr. famously said, "Injustice anywhere is a threat to justice everywhere. We are caught in an inescapable network of mutuality, tied in a single garment of destiny. Whatever affects one directly, affects all indirectly". This web of mutuality obligates us to care for all humans, no matter how near or far. There are ideas woven in to this way of thinking about the importance of reciprocity, solidarity, and equality. Now some will argue that we only owe an obligation of care for those who are nearby or to those who can reciprocate. But others will even extend this to include beings who cannot reciprocate: such as nonhuman animals. Authors such as Albert Schweitzer extended reverence for life in a way that includes far more than human life. And in some Buddhist texts, there is a call to show compassion to all sentient beings.

But even ardent vegetarians will have to confront the question of "to whom?" when dealing with pests —rats or mosquitoes— who invade the house or garden. It turns out that it is not easy to provide a coherent answer to the question of "to whom?" The world includes predation —as well as crime, war, and a history of racism and exploitation. Nonetheless, the prevailing idea among advocates of nonviolence is that we should strive, as much as possible, to extend the circle of concern in order to avoid the kind of privilege and hierarchy that are at the heart of both direct/overt violence and structural/systematic violence. Albert Einstein, who was an ardent pacifist, supposedly said in a widely-quoted passage that we need to look beyond the delusion of our separateness and that "our task must be to free ourselves from this prison by widening our circle of compassion to embrace all living creatures and the whole of nature in its beauty". Another famous Albert, the pacifist doctor Albert Schweitzer, suggested that we ought to expand the circle of compassion under the rubric of "reverence for life". Schweitzer explained that "the circle of ethics always grows wider, and ethics becomes more profound... The circle described by ethics is always widening".

More recently, Peter Singer wrote a book called *The Expanding Circle*, where he made a similar argument. Michael W. Fox put it this way in a book called *The Boundless Circle*: "the modern hero is surely one who actively affirms ahimsa in both professional and personal realms and, rather than remaining passive or indifferent toward the myriad crimes of violence against creatures and Creation, seeks every means to expand the principle of compassionate protection of all life where it is needed... It is not a question of drawing some arbitrary line as to which creatures and to what extent we should exploit them. Rather, we should draw a circle, a boundless circle of compassion to include all creatures and Creation within the scope of our respect and reverence". This could be another way of defining nonviolence, as a boundless circle of compassion or an expanding circle of respect and reverence for life.

The Power of the Powerless

The tradition of nonviolence is often understood as a counter-narrative to the traditions of violence associated with social and political power. The just war tradition, mentioned above, provides a set of criteria for thinking about the justification of using violence in the international arena. These ideas can also be used to clarify thinking about justifying police violence, the death penalty, and so on. The nonviolent tradition is not primarily concerned with the question of when or how violence can be justified. One reason for this could be that nonviolence may merely be the method and strategy of those who lack weapons and do not have the means to engage in successful violence. In this sense, nonviolence is not primarily a moral choice; rather, it is a practical alternative for those who lack the capacity to engage in violence. Ackerman and DuVall put it this way: "It is often assumed that the choice of nonviolent resistance is made for moral reasons, but the historical record suggests otherwise. Most who used nonviolent actions in the twentieth century did so because military or physical force was not a viable action". Ackerman and DuVall show that nonviolence has been effective. But they point out that the choice of nonviolence is pragmatic: it is a choice made out of an assessment of the risks of using violence and the likelihood of success. In this regard, nonviolence may be understood merely as a tool for the powerless to employ in fighting against power on behalf of the marginalized and oppressed. In a sense, nonviolence is the "power of the powerless" to borrow a phrase from Vaclav Havel, the dissident who became President of Czechoslovakia after the Velvet Revolution of 1989.

But we must be careful with this formulation. On the one hand, this patronizing description subtly marginalizes and discredits those who engage in nonviolence —as if the powerless somehow lack the will to fight or lack courage and so on. Nonviolence also has a moral component that goes beyond mere pragmatics. The advocates of nonviolence in the nonviolent tradition do not call for nonviolence simply *because* they lack access to power, as if they would give up their commitment to nonviolence once they gain power and are able to employ violence with impunity. Rather, the advocates of nonviolence think that it is morally superior and more effective than violence in bringing about morally acceptable outcomes. The advocates of nonviolence do not understand it as a tool that is only of use for the powerless. In fact they often imagine a transformation of social and political power in general, in the direction of nonviolence —so that even the powerful would limit their use of violence. In a sense, the dream of nonviolence is of a world transformed in such a way that the discrepancy between the powerful and the powerless fades away so that nonviolence becomes the primary mode of social and political interaction in a world committed to truth, love, and justice. Recent calls in the U.S. to "defund the police" are part of this idea, as well as calls for prison abolition.

Not everyone who struggles against powerful and oppressive systems is an advocate of nonviolence. There are others such as Malcolm X and Frantz

Fanon who call for violence in such struggles. Malcolm is well-known for the phrase "by any means necessary": he said he and his organization wanted freedom, justice, and equality "by any means necessary". He called upon the African American community to defend itself against violence. He said in a speech in 1964, "The time for you and me to allow ourselves to be brutalized nonviolently is passé. Be nonviolent only with those who are nonviolent to you". The proponents of nonviolence, of course, think differently: they insist on employing nonviolence most (or all) of the time, even in response to those who are violent. Malcolm's claim is about self-defense. But it was also about self-respect in a racist society that allowed whites to use violence against Blacks, while systematically dis-arming Blacks. Malcolm claimed that the use of violence by Blacks is only a matter of equality and justice: Blacks should have the same power to use violence as whites (and the white racist police and authorities of the Jim Crow era). For Blacks to refuse violence in such a situation would be for Blacks to agree to submit to this kind of inequality and disempowerment.

A further point is made by Fanon: that when the powerless and marginalized avoid violence, they give up on a tool that is not only effective but also symbolically liberating. Fanon suggested that when colonized people turn to violence it is not their fault. Rather, this is what he called the "boomerang" of violence —the violence of the oppressor turned against itself. Fanon said decolonization is always violent, since it erupts from out of the background condition of violence. But more importantly, it is through violence that those who struggle for liberation prove to the world and to themselves that they are human beings. Fanon writes that those who struggle for liberation are working "towards the death of the colonist". He continues, "The colonized man liberates himself in and through violence. This praxis enlightens the militant because it shows him the means and the end". Sartre reiterated this in his Preface to Fanon's *The Wretched of the Earth*, that those who advocate for nonviolence fail to understand that the whole structure is rotten and that there is something self-serving and hypocritical about the call for nonviolence coming from those who benefit from and who are steeped in violence. This critique was taken up more recently by Ward Churchill and others who suggest that nonviolence is a "pathology of the privileged", something that the oppressor calls for; and if oppressed people call for nonviolence that may be because they have been brainwashed in such a way that they identify with the oppressor and his call for nonviolence.

In response to these critiques, advocates of nonviolence have offered a number of responses. First, proponents of nonviolence will argue that nonviolence is more practically effective than violence —especially for those who are systematically disempowered. In a contest of arms between the state and a minority group, the state will usually win. Along with this argument, proponents of nonviolence will claim that what is needed is creative nonviolence that actually works by employing multiple tactics informed by a growing science of nonviolence. Second, proponents of nonviolence will appeal to moral arguments, which claim nonviolence is morally superior to violence. A third response is the claim that nonviolence comes out of a deep and coherent tradition —such as a religious tradition.

These responses —the practical, the moral, and the religious— help to show that nonviolence is not merely a pathetic last resort for powerless people. At the practical level, if the goal is to generate social and political change in order to transform the system of power and disempowerment, then nonviolence can be the wise and prudent choice. This is not always true. But one must be strategic about social movements and revolutionary transformation. The proponents of violence often celebrate violence because of its emotionally satisfying power. It feels good to strike out against enemies. Violence satisfies emotions such as anger and resentment. It also leaves a mark and makes a statement. But if violence incurs reprisals and escalation of oppression, then it not a useful tool. Furthermore, the developed strategies of nonviolence are not merely pleas for pity; they can be coercive and powerful. With regard to the moral level, as we have been arguing throughout, there is a vision of a better world woven into nonviolence, which is egalitarian, democratic, and just. In pursuit of long-term transformation of social and political life, this vision of a better world provides inspiration and a North Star that guides actions in the near and long term. This vision is also inclusive, allowing for former enemies to reconcile in the name of a world transformed for the better. Finally, with regard to religious traditions, it is worth noting that most of the world's traditions emphasize nonviolence and celebrate peace. There is a coherent global story about the need to beat plowshares into swords, whether we call it *pax, shalom, salaam,* or *ahimsa.*

It is true that nonviolent religion can seem to be a minority position. And some of the important voices in this tradition are marginalized and powerless, which reiterates the problem of whether nonviolence should be understood as merely the power of the powerless. But there are efforts underway to transform mainstream religious and moral traditions in a more nonviolent direction. The Catholic church has come to embrace a kind of pacifism in its call for a consistent ethic of life that is opposed to abortion, euthanasia, suicide, the death penalty, and war. This transformation is remarkable given the history of the church's advocacy for the death penalty and its central role in crusading wars and the development of the just war tradition. This transformation of Catholicism shows us that nonviolence is not merely for the powerless. Similar reinterpretations have occurred in other contexts. For example, Islamic scholars have worked to demonstrate Muslim commitment to nonviolence and peace. And in political life across the globe, there has been substantial movement in the direction of nonviolence: the death penalty is gradually being abolished, domestic violence and sexual violence has been put under a microscope, corporal punishment in the schools has been radically changed, and an international system has developed that is aimed at preventing and limiting war. It seems obvious that nonviolence is no longer merely an expedient for the powerless. It is growing in value even for the powerful.

Normal Nonviolence and the Constructive Program

Nonviolence is much larger than the question of how oppressed people might create a social and political revolution. The revolutionary context is more glamorous and spectacular. Revolutionary action puts the issue of nonviolence into stark relief, as forces of nonviolence stand up against the state's monopoly of violence. Revolutionaries are inspirational and heroic figures. But there is also a less glamorous and more widespread kind of nonviolence: the nonviolence of ordinary life and a positive vision of nonviolent life. This is connected to the constructive program that aims to create nonviolent social life here and now.

There are substantial parts of our lives that are simply not violent —when we are working, playing, thinking, making art, and so on. Predrag Cicovacki puts it this way in explaining how Gandhi and Schweitzer understood nonviolence as a "way of life": "If we consider our usual daily behavior, we notice that, in the vast majority of cases, people behave nonviolently toward each other. Hundreds of nations also live in peace, but history ignores these facts and records only wars and quarrels". The *normal* life of a business, a family, a city, or a nation is often nonviolent (or ought to be). There are occasional outbursts of violence: domestic violence, work-place violence, crime, and war. But these are anomalous malfunctions of social life. Once these abnormal malfunctions are fixed, the goal is to return to normal, nonviolent life: to get back to working, playing, educating, and living.

As Cicovacki points out, this is even true at the international level. Of course so-called realists will disagree. Inspired by insights found in the work of Thomas Hobbes and Carl von Clausewitz, realists claim that the international arena is structured by war, which is basically "politics by other means". But there is a rival theory according to which international peace spreads as democracy, human rights, trade, capitalism, and the rule of law develops. These ideas —variously called the democratic peace theory, the capitalist peace theory, or the theory of liberal internationalism— have roots in the thinking of enlightenment thinkers such as Immanuel

Kant, Adam Smith and the Baron de Montesquieu. Indeed, there is evidence that in both domestic and international affairs, the world is becoming less violent. Steven Pinker has provided extensive empirical and historical evidence that shows that violence decreases as capitalism, globalization, and technology make people happier, healthier, and less inclined to violence. Pinker links peace to a rising standard of living: prosperity causes violence to decrease since "Richer countries, on average, fight fewer wars with each other, are less likely to be riven by civil wars, are more likely to become and stay democratic, and have greater respect for human rights". Prosperity itself results from capitalism, commerce, technological innovation, moral development, stable social systems, representational/democratic politics, and other innovations developed under the general rubric of what Pinker calls "Enlightenment".

Even purveyors of violence are nonviolent most of the time. The committed sadist does not spend all of his day destroying things: he sleeps, eats, buys groceries, and obeys the traffic rules. An institution such as a concentration camp can be understood as a non-stop industrial-level violent operation. But even within structures and institutions of violence, there is a kind of quotidian nonviolence among the guards and purveyors of violence. This is something like what Hannah Arendt described in terms of the banality of evil. The problem of institutional and structural violence is that from a certain vantage point, it looks normal. A slave society does not consist of 24-7 beating and whipping. Once slavery is normalized, there is a kind of nonviolence that holds within the system and between the threats, beatings, and brutality. This is, in fact, why critics of structural violence will focus on the need for critical engagement and radical change: we often do not see structural violence because on the surface, things have a veneer of nonviolence.

At issue here are questions of power, identity, and the directionality of violence. Consider the case of racial and other forms of social violence, including both overt racial violence and more subtle forms of racialized structural violence. While racists participate in violence against the racialized other, the racist is nonviolent toward members of his own race. Violence directed against the other is understood as an effort to exclude or eliminate the other from the in-group. The in-group is understood in terms of its own privileged, internally directed nonviolence. Indeed, in hierarchical and unequal societies that contain structural violence, the institutions and systems of power are put in place, oddly enough, to eliminate overt violence. The goal of structural violence is actually a kind of nonviolence. Of course this is perverse, ideologically fraught, and seemingly incoherent. But to acknowledge this is to understand the problem that leads to the claims of normative nonviolence. It would be better, the advocates of nonviolence argue, for everyone to practice nonviolence all of the time in relation to everyone else. And, of course, it would be better if structural violence were eliminated and everyone could participate equally in the goods of nonviolence, which the ruling class or dominant race preserves for itself.

In a system of structural violence, the veneer of nonviolence creates a sphere of immunity from violence, which makes it difficult to see the violence lurking beneath the surface. The ruling class or race practices nonviolence most of the time toward those who it views as social equals and who are thus immune from violence. But "the other" is not given protection within the circle of privileged immunity. This problem occurs even within democratic nations. Citizens enjoy protections which non-citizens do not. Those of us lucky enough to enjoy the privileges of the developed world's capitalist economy ignore, for example, the violence (the destructive force) that occurs in the global economy, including the exploitative labor practices that fuel the consumer society. A similar failure appears when we extend our thinking about who deserves immunity from violence to include nonhuman animals. A carnivorous diet depends upon a system of industrialized violence against animals. But meat-eaters (if we accept that this is violence) are generally nonviolent toward members of the human species. Now a carnivore may complain that this is not violence, perhaps arguing that animals are not moral patients who are worthy of moral consideration. But our basic definition of violence would clearly include violence toward animals: to kill and consume an animal body is clearly to deliberately destroy it. But —and here is my point— the meat-eater's identity, spirit, or soul is not tied up in the fundamental violence that feeds his body; he views this violence as normal. Most meat-eaters love their families and avoid fighting. They are nonviolent most of the time, despite ongoing participation in a system of violence. This example may seem perverse, since meat-eating is taken for granted as normal. But the example shows that the question of violence is woven deep into the structures of our lives and the issue of what counts as normal.

Comprehensive nonviolence includes what Gandhi called a "constructive program" for nonviolent social life. The goal is to unwind structures of violence and to build a social system that is kinder, gentler, more humane, and less destructive. The resources for imagining such a constructive program are grounded in a claim about the normal nonviolence of life. There are many models for this. Gandhi's constructive program included, for example, weaving cloth, seeking communal unity across religious differences, removing untouchability in the caste system, prohibition of intoxicants, equality for women, sanitation, education, hygiene, and so on. Gandhi's vision of social transformation was much broader than a protest movement against British rule. He thought that if Indians united around this program, they would be more successful against the British. He also thought that his constructive program represented a vision for a good, nonviolent life once the British had left.

A different vision can be found in the Christian tradition. As noted, one frequently cited source of the tradition of nonviolence is Jesus's "Sermon on the Mount" (Matthew 5-7). In that text, as well as the related text from Luke called the "Sermon on the Plain" (Luke 6), Jesus celebrates the nonviolence of ordinary life. The most famous passage offers a reinterpretation of the old law of *lex talionis*, saying that we should not return evil for evil, that we should turn the other cheek, and that we should love our enemies. But prior to offering these proposals for radical nonviolence, Jesus gives us a list of good things, known as "the beatitudes". Jesus lists eight things that are blessed: poverty, meekness, mournfulness, hunger/thirst, mercy, cleanness/purity, suffering, and peacemaking. These are the virtues, activities, and character traits of people who are the "salt of the earth", as Jesus says. Jesus's point is not merely to argue against violence and retributive justice. Rather, he calls for what we would call today "restorative justice" as well as "social justice". Jesus's message is a protest against Empire; but he also offers a vision of a nonviolent community where it is normal to care for the poor and the weak, where people are merciful and forgiving, where the naked are clothed, and the unhoused are given homes.

The combined vision of Gandhi and Jesus helped to influence the constructive program associated with the American civil rights movements. Activists were involved in registering people to vote, distributing basic resources, and supporting local Black communities in the South in their struggle against Jim Crow. James Lawson, one of the leaders of this effort, has said that to live nonviolently is to live as a citizen of a country that does not yet exist. He means that we ought to live here and now as if nonviolence were widespread and normal. As a result we will live in a way that transforms the world. Lawson identifies the four evils of the contemporary world as racism, militarism, plantation capitalism, and sexism. To live nonviolently is to live without racial prejudice, without resort to violence, without rapacity and greed, and without sexual violence and inequality. Lawson reminds us that nonviolence is ultimately up to us. We have the choice, right now, to live without sexism, racism, and the like. This choice is a choice about ordinary life and what we take to be normal. It involves all our relations with family, friends, neighbors, and colleagues. It influences how we vote, what we read, where we shop, and so on. Consider, for example, how the nonviolent Catholic activist John Dear has turned his attention to ecological issues. He has called for a constructive program of ecologically sustainable nonviolent culture. This would include projects in schools, churches, and communities such as food coops, educational centers, financial coops, interfaith initiatives, and health care projects.

In concluding this section, the point is this: nonviolence extends to the way we live our lives and what we take for granted as normal. The goods of life are nonviolent. We enjoy them on a daily basis: work, play, love, thought, and so on. But often violence interferes. We should seek to prevent such violent interference (to prevent crime and domestic violence, for example). And when it does occur, we should seek to restore normal life and community. This involves a critique of structural violence and a positive effort, or constructive program, that helps each of us live more nonviolently right here and right now.

The Social Ontology and Moral Psychology of Nonviolence

The questions of "who" and "to whom" leads us to consider the theory of social life and of the self that is central to the philosophy of nonviolence. There are two points of view here: that of the individual and that of society.

Let's begin with individuals and consider the psychological dynamics, character traits, and virtues at work in nonviolence. What kinds of people are nonviolent and what are the characteristics of a peaceful person? When viewed from an individualistic standpoint, there are virtues, dispositions, and habits that are typical of nonviolent personalities. Some of these virtues have been highlighted in the pacifist traditions of the world. Jesus, for example, calls for mercy, forgiveness, and toleration. In other traditions, such as Buddhism, there is a focus on what we might simplistically call "inner peace". In the developed philosophy and practice of contemporary nonviolence it is common to suggest that nonviolence requires substantial "inner work" along with education, training, and discipline. This is true both in terms of the nonviolence of ordinary life and in the more politically focused strategic work of nonviolent activists.

To get an idea of the internalist or "inner peace" approach, consider the Dalai Lama's Nobel Peace Prize address, where he stated that "Peace starts with each one of us. When we have inner peace, we can be at peace with those around us". The Dalai Lama lists a number of values that promote inner peace: love, kindness, happiness, and care. These are related to the other sorts of traits and dispositions that empirical psychologists have identified as characteristics of peaceful people.

Peace Psychology

In a summary of the empirical research, Daniel Mayton provides a useful overview of peaceful traits and nonviolent dispositions. This research develops out of the work of so-called "positive psychology" (which focuses on positive traits instead of on negative or dysfunctional traits).

Some of the following traits are clearly supported by the research; others are merely suggested by the literature on nonviolence. The traits of a nonviolent person include:

- agreeableness
- anger control
- empathy
- need for cognition (taking joy in thinking)
- spirituality (belief in a higher power)
- rejection of materialism
- optimism (hopefulness)
- forgiveness and mercy
- happiness
- prudence
- self-regulation
- perspective taking
- open-mindedness (tolerance)
- kindness

More research needs to be done in the field of peace psychology. And we need more work on programs for educating and training people in these virtues, traits, and dispositions, i.e., in the field of peace education. But much work has already been done. And we should note that nonviolent spiritual traditions such as Buddhism already have centuries of practice at working to cultivate inner peace through meditation and the practice of mindfulness.

The philosophy of nonviolence changes our understanding of the self and its relation to the social world. The virtues of nonviolent persons are not merely individual achievements or possessions. Rather, the philosophy of nonviolence points in the direction of a conception of the self that is interconnected with other selves and a view of society that stresses interdependence. The connection between inner peace and a transformed vision of society and the world has been articulated, for example, by Black Elk, the Lakota holy man. Black Elk explained that there were three levels of peace: internal peace, peace with other persons, and peace among nations. He said, "there can never be peace between nations until there is first known that true peace which is within the souls of men".

4. The Dalai Lama in Dharamsala, India.

Nonviolence asks us to think about the social world in a way that is more integrated and less individualistic. The proponents of nonviolence tend to think that persons are interrelated and that the distinction between self and other should be transformed in a way that gives us a more social view of the self. This includes a critique of hierarchical social structures that lead to oppression and domination. This point has been made recently by Judith Butler, who explains that nonviolence points in the direction of equality and interdependence. She argues, "an ethics of nonviolence cannot be predicated on individualism, and it must take the lead in waging a critique of individualism". Butler imagines that the philosophy of nonviolence would result in a radical shift in our way of thinking about bodies, relationships, and ethical obligations.

A similar idea can be found in the writings of Gandhi and King. King said "all men are brothers", as we explained above. In order to avoid hierarchical, racist, and gendered language, we might ought rather say, "all beings are interrelated". But let's stick with King, as our exemplar. When he claims that "If you harm me, you harm yourself" this shows us the depth of the social ontology of nonviolence. King suggests that the web of interdependence and interrelation is so deep that injury, violence, and harm are shared by all of us. King's ideas depend upon the ideal concept of "the beloved community", which is the name for a community that recognizes this type of deep interconnection. King grounds this idea in Christian thought about love and the kingdom of God. But he also appeals to ideas found in Gandhi. Gandhi's ideal builds upon what he calls the "law of love". This is the power that helps organize family life in accord with nonviolence, a power that Gandhi extends toward a broader conception of the human family, where "the of law of love" is the key to resolving disputes. Gandhi explained how this idea would transform concretely social relationships, for example, with regard to untouchability in the Indian caste system. Gandhi held out the hope that there would be a transformation of the social, political, and religious stigma of untouchability. But he explained, "I very much fear that we are a long way from that bright and happy day when we shall be all masters and no servants, or all servants and no masters, all members of the human family, regarding ourselves as blood–brothers and blood–sisters".

This idea shows us the agenda of the transformed social ontology of nonviolence. The ideal is a world in which there are no servants and no masters and in which we view ourselves as members of the human family, as brothers and sisters. This metaphor may even be extended beyond the human family to include the idea that all beings are interconnected and interdependent.

The spirit of nonviolence has had a profound impact on the development of ecology. Among the most influential thinkers in the movement known as "deep ecology" is Arne Naess, the Norwegian philosopher whose work follows closely upon ideas he developed from his reading of Gandhi. Naess explained, "Gandhi made manifest the internal relationship between self-realization, nonviolence, and what has sometimes been called biospherical egalitarianism". Biospherical egalitarianism is another way of referring to the transformed ontology of nonviolence, although in this case we move beyond social ontology oriented toward human society and begin to think of a revised notion of society, as a society of all beings. Nonviolence and ecology point toward a larger theory of interconnection and interdependence. This means we must revise our understanding of individualism and the self. Naess explains this further by invoking the notion of a "wider self" that is connected to the idea of "the essential oneness of all life". There is a clear echo here of ideas found in the Hindu and Jain traditions. In the Vedanta school of Hindu thought, the claim is made that "Atman is Brahman", which means that the individual self or soul is connected to or identified with the world soul or cosmic self. Similar ideas about the interconnection of things can be found in other of the world's religious traditions.

A clear statement of this transformed way of thinking about the relation between self and other is found in Jesus and the Jewish tradition he inherited, which says we should love our neighbors as ourselves (Leviticus 19:18; Matthew 22:39). This idea is known as the Golden Rule. The Golden Rule opens the door to a transformative social ontology, such that the neighbor is viewed as another self, worthy of the same love that we give to ourselves.

Versions of the Golden Rule are found in many of the world's traditions. For example, we see it in Confucianism and in Taoism, as well as in Buddhism, and other traditions. One inspiring example is found in the writings of Mozi (or Mo Tzu) who advocated an ethic of mutual love. He wrote: "When all the people in the world love one another, then the strong will not overpower the weak, the many will not oppress the few, the wealthy will not mock the poor, the honoured will not disdain the humble, and the cunning will not deceive the simple. And it is all due to mutual love that calamities, strife, complaints, and hatred are prevented from arising". Mozi outlines here a recipe for positive peace: a world without war, strife, and oppression; a world of love, harmony, and peace.

To say that we should love our neighbors as ourselves asks us to imagine an intimate connection between self and other. Not only does it ask us to imagine the circumstances of the other, but this also asks us to rethink ideas about personal property, relationships, community, and political life. The other person's life has the same value as one's own.

This leads to a general ethic of loving kindness, compassion, and charity that transforms our thinking about self and other. Beneath this is a vision of the kind of revised social ontology we have been describing.

If someone needs something, we ought to give it to them —because their lack affects us. The suffering of the other matters because we are interconnected: if the other is suffering, then so am I. In a world of individualism and private property, there is a sense that each of us is on our own, struggling to survive. But a radically different idea develops if we look beyond individualism toward mutual dependence and begin to understand our essential interconnectedness. The vision of social life that emerges here is one in which self and other are intimately related and in which the ordinary understanding of individualism and private property is radically transformed.

This may sound like a crazy idea. But the metaphor guiding this shows that it is not completely absurd: i.e., the metaphor of family life and "the domestic analogy" of pacifism, which holds that we are all brothers and sisters. This revised idea of social life asks us to revise individualistic ways of thinking about self, other, and the world. Such a transformation would be facilitated by peace psychology and the character traits of a peaceful person; and, in turn, a transformed social ontology would help to support the development of those characteristics.

Nonviolence for the Powerful

Nonviolence has often been described as a kind of power for the powerless, a method to be employed by those who lack social and political power. But nonviolence can also be employed by the powerful. Indeed, the best way to create a more peaceful world is for the powerful to be less violent. The change of social ontology imagined by nonviolence makes this point clear. If we are going to create a world in which there are no slaves and no masters, we need to persuade the masters to relinquish their monopoly on violence. The result should be a change in the way that social power is organized and distributed. When nonviolence triumphs, all members of society would work to develop those characteristics of peaceful persons we described above (agreeableness, mercy, and so on). Society would also find ways to de-escalate conflict and to change the way that power is deployed.

One example will suffice, I hope, to explain how nonviolence might change institutional power: the example of restorative justice. Restorative justice provides a nonviolent alternative to the typical violence found in traditional systems of criminal justice. When people advocate for defunding the police or for abolition of prisons, they often turn to restorative justice as a replacement for maintaining social order.

In traditional approaches to criminal justice, the police, the courts, and the prisons possess a monopoly on the use of violence. The cops shoot, beat, and arrest people —and often do so with a kind of impunity granted to them by society in the name of law and order. The courts can compel testimony (including the use of physical torture and psychological violence, which was typical of pre-modern "inquisitions" but which also returned under the rubric of "enhanced interrogation" in the U.S. war on terrorism). Once a verdict is reached, the criminal justice system uses force and the threat of violence to confine criminals to prison. In some cases, the violence of corporal punishment is deployed, including the ultimate violence of the death penalty.

The violence of this system is thought to be justified in two ways: (1) by utilitarian arguments about deterring and preventing crime; and (2) by a more deontological account of retributive justice. Retributive justice is tightly connected with violence, resting as it does on the idea of "eye for eye" and "life for life", which is really another way of saying "violence should be responded to with violence". Utilitarian arguments about deterrence and prevention also do not mind using violence as part of this process, believing that the end (of reducing crime) can justify the means (of using violence to deter and prevent crime).

The nonviolent alternative to retributive justice and to violent deterrence/prevention is known as restorative justice. A closely related and emerging idea is called relational justice. Restorative justice aims to restore and rebuild —rather than to retaliate. Relational justice seeks to heal relationships by listening to, caring for, and supporting everyone who suffers under crime and violence —including victims, perpetrators, and the rest of the community. These alternative ideas about criminal justice do not ignore or downplay the impact of crime. Nor do they tell us to "forgive and forget". It is not possible to imagine a *system* of justice that focuses on forgiveness, which seems more like a personal or individual choice than a systematic approach to justice. Rather than forgiveness, the goal in restorative justice is better described as to "remember and heal". In restorative justice, harms are acknowledged. But instead of "punishing" those crimes (where punishment is understood as the usage of violence), the goal is to provide healing, remediation, reconciliation, rehabilitation, and restoration. Rather than using violence against perpetrators of crime, restorative justice wants to find ways to bring victims and perpetrators together, to rebuild broken relationships, and to find ways to heal and restore the community.

This idea has been employed with success in schools and in dealing with juveniles. The easiest examples of restorative justice focus on nonviolent offenses, such as property crime. Restorative justice may be more difficult with regard to violent crimes such as rape and murder. Some would argue, more forcefully, that it would be wrong to employ restorative justice in the case of violent crime. But there is also some evidence to show that victims of violent crime can benefit from restorative efforts, which help to empower them and validate their experience in a way that other forms of criminal justice do not.

Restorative models have also been put into practice in the aftermath of large scale social and political violence. The most famous case is South Africa's "Truth and Reconciliation" process (led by Desmond Tutu), which has provided a model for other truth and reconciliation commissions in other countries. The methods and goals of restorative justice include publicly acknowledging the truth of wrongdoing and harm, holding wrong-doers accountable (without understanding accountability only in terms of liability for violent punishment), finding ways to repair damage and make amends, and supporting and empowering victims of wrongdoing. Howard Zehr, a leading advocate for restorative justice, explains that the practice depends upon the 3 R's of respect, responsibility, and relationship.

5. Samuel L. Jackson and Desmond Tutu at the celebration of Archbishop Desmond Tutu's 75th birthday held at the Regent Beverly Wilshire Hotel in Beverly Hills, USA on September 18, 2006.

Furthermore, we should mention that restorative justice —which happens after a crime has occurred— is often considered in conjunction with other more proactive efforts at reconciliation and mediation that seek to prevent harm, de-escalate conflict, reduce polarization, and generally encourage positive relationships. Under consideration here are efforts at community dialogue, shared arts and sports projects, educational efforts, and so on, which are intended to reduce hate, while preventing violence. Such efforts are sometimes described as "peace-building" or "peace-making" projects. These preventive efforts, in combination with restorative justice practices, are ways that the structures of power can become less violent.

There is much more to be said about these nonviolent alternatives. But the point here has been to highlight one of the ways that we might transform structures of power in a nonviolent direction. A variety of other topics could be considered in relation to nonviolence for the powerful including: nonviolent weapon and tactics in the military, nonviolent policing, nonviolent pedagogies, nonviolent economics, and nonviolent childrearing. Structures of power —from the military to the schools, the economy and the family— can be made less violent. Nonviolence is thus not only a tactic employed by the powerless as they protest social injustice and political power. It can also be conceived as a set of principles and practices that could be used by the powerful and woven into structures of power.

Chapter 4

The How and Why of Nonviolence

In this chapter, we will consider the role of nonviolence in struggles for power, while discussing why and how nonviolence should be employed in social movements. Among the key ideas to be discussed here are: how nonviolence transforms the power differential, the difference between principled and pragmatic approaches to nonviolence, the importance of nonviolence in democracy, and the connection between nonviolence and critiques of power. We will also discuss methods of social protest and extra-institutional politics, as well as the continuum of strategies of nonviolence including civil disobedience.

Moral and Political Jiu-Jitsu

Empirical studies show that nonviolence is often more effective than violence. It is not always effective (no method of action always works) but it tends to work. Why is that? One answer has to do with the coordination of means and ends in nonviolence, especially in relation to democratic values. Nonviolence tends to work to promote human rights, social justice, and other democratic values because it embodies these values in the methods it employs. But before exploring the democratic power of nonviolence, let's consider another explanation often found in discussions of nonviolence: the idea of nonviolence as moral or political jiu-jitsu. The basic idea, imported from Asian martial arts, is to use an opponent's force against him. Actual jiu-jitsu evolved as a technique by which a weak, unarmed combatant could respond to aggressive attacks by stronger, armed opponents. The techniques involve deflecting attacks, redirecting the thrust of an attack, and using the opponent's own power and momentum to throw the opponent off balance. Jiu-jitsu helps a less powerful person respond to and manipulate a more powerful person. This basic concept has been used to describe the way that nonviolence works in the political arena by both Richard Gregg and Gene Sharp.

Richard Gregg was an American who popularized Gandhian methods, beginning in the 1930's. Gregg's book, *The Power of Nonviolence* (originally published in 1935) was read by Martin Luther King Jr., when King was a student. King wrote a Forward to the third edition of the book that Gregg published in 1958. Two points should be emphasized: (1) Gregg suggests that nonviolent jiu-jitsu must come from a place of psychological and spiritual wisdom or enlightenment and (2) Gregg acknowledges that one of the most powerful components of nonviolence is the idea of "voluntary suffering". In explaining why this works, Gregg suggested that those who employ violence expect that their attacks will be responded to with violence. The purveyors of violence view the world through a lens of violence. They are prepared to respond to violence with more violence. The aggressor's goal in such an encounter is to establish supremacy, understood as domination through physical force. Gregg explained that nonviolence uses the assumption of violence to disarm those who are violent by refusing to respond to violence with violence. This is what Gregg calls "moral jiu-jitsu". There is an element of surprise in nonviolence that throws the violent attacker off-balance, when the nonviolent actor refuses to engage in violence. The violent attacker is ready to handle a violent response. In fact, the attacker may actually *want* a violent response, since this would enable the attacker to demonstrate his superior violent power. But a nonviolent response changes the subject —away from physical supremacy and toward a consideration of moral values. Voluntary suffering comes into play here as a way of demonstrating the nonviolent person's commitment to those values. One of the ways that nonviolence is supposed to work on this account is that the attacker comes to understand that it is fruitless to attack one who will not respond with violence and who is not deterred by the threat of further violence.

All of this gets combined with the negative effect that a one-sided violent onslaught has on spectators, third parties, and public opinion. During the Black Lives Matter protests of 2020, when the police attacked nonviolent protestors, support for those protests grew. Indeed, the violence of the police served to demonstrate the very thing being protested, which was police brutality (especially police brutality used against unarmed Black people). When a political protest becomes violent, it is easy to blame the protestors for inciting that violence. But, as David Cortright puts it, "as a general rule, nonviolence attracts support, while violence repels it". That's why it is necessary for agents of nonviolence to remain steadfast and consistent in their nonviolence. While it is tempting to resort to violence and lash out in response to violence, the resort to violence can undermine the goodwill that is generated among third parties, as well as among potential defectors from the dominant group. This occurred in 2020, for example, when looting and arson occurred during the BLM protests. Looting tends to turn off potential supporters, who are likely to see the violence of the protests as a threat.

Consider a schematic example of a protest involving two rival groups, Group A and Group B. The protest begins with Group A occupying a public space, waving signs, chanting, and so on. Counter-protesters from Group B show up and respond. The police are also involved, supervising the space. Now imagine that B provokes A into a fight. Members of A respond. Fists are flying all around. The police wade into the crowd. Members of both A and B respond to each other and to the police. Violence is turned against the police. Violence escalates. Tear gas is deployed. Members of both A and B are arrested. Spectators and bystanders will want to assign blame. The police will blame both parties. It will be difficult to trace back the causal story and figure out who threw the first punch. At any rate, the question of who threw the first punch will be overshadowed by the frenzy of the general conflagration. And the issue that Group A was protesting about will be overshadowed by the violence of the event. The court system and the media will focus on the violence —and will ignore the original issue.

Now if this scenario changes and Group A responds nonviolently to the provocations of Group B things might turn out differently. Group B will be exposed as a violent group of bullies. And if the police crackdown on the violence, they will be coming to the aid of Group A by arresting members of Group B. This will portray the issue that Group A is advancing in a more positive light.

Now let's change the scenario again, this time with the police rounding up members of both A and B. Imagine that Group B, which is committed to violence, fights back and resists the power of the police. Violence will escalate and Group B will again be discredited in the eyes of the public. They will be described as terrorists or anarchists for fighting against the police. Now imagine that the nonviolent members of Group A allow themselves to be arrested without fighting back. Perhaps they even suffer beatings and rough treatment at the hands of the police, while refusing to fight back. This will send a different message. Imagine even that the political establishment tries to portray Group A as yet another group of anarchists or terrorists. But the images of the police attacking nonviolent protesters will prove this to be false.

The notion of voluntary suffering is one of the difficult sticking points in the theory and practice of nonviolence. Critics of nonviolence will argue that there is something wrong about not fighting back in such cases either against the assaults of the rival group or against the police. Ardent defenders of the right to self-defense will argue that individuals who are under attack have a right to fight back. Some will even say that to not fight back is to exhibit cowardice or to lack self-respect. Defenders of nonviolence will respond in various ways to this criticism. Some advocates of nonviolence connect voluntary suffering to a larger metaphysical scheme. Some may suggest that there is something like "karma" at work in the universe: a system of cause and effect that ensures that when good people are assaulted, there is a long-term process that balances out harms and benefits. In the Christian tradition, there is an idea of divine judgment that works in a similar fashion. Martin Luther King once explained that "unearned suffering is redemptive". He connected this to ideas he found in Gandhi, who said that things of fundamental importance have to be purchased with suffering. For a Christian like King, this idea can be easily connected to the model of Christ, whose death on the cross provided redemption from sin. But one need not be a Christian to accept a less metaphysical interpretation of the power of voluntary suffering. Bystanders and third parties can be induced to pick sides when watching powerful bullies cruelly attack nonviolent persons. This can also have a positive impact on members of a protest group who may develop a stronger sense of solidarity and be inspired to work harder when members of their group suffer from violence.

Gene Sharp updated Gregg's idea of moral jiu-jitsu, calling it "political jiu-jitsu". According to Sharp, political power rests upon the consent of the governed. When political parties employ violence against nonviolent protesters, this serves to undermine this structure of consent, as people come to see the state as an oppressive entity. Sharp says, "Nonviolent struggle has the potential to make a government powerless". Sharp implies that when the state has to resort to violence, its power is often already tenuous. When this violence is responded to with nonviolence —and when sympathy and solidarity for the nonviolent movement grows— the state finds itself in a precarious situation. In a political system that involves substantial support of the people, there is little need for violence: the people comply and obey because they believe that the system is working on their behalf and for their interest; they also share a basic agreement about values. But in an oppressive system that does not rest upon that kind of support, the state will resort to violence to establish its power, expecting conformity as a result. The state may be able to justify its violence in response to violent opposition by claiming a need for security and "law and order". But such claims fall flat when the opposition is nonviolent. Thus nonviolence can expose the state's moral and political bankruptcy. The ordinary and more stable source of power (in the consent of the governed) is lacking when there is a substantial protest movement. And the state's calls for "law and order" are unpersuasive when the opposition remains nonviolent.

The Democratic Power of Nonviolence

The ideal conception of political power at work in nonviolence is fundamentally democratic. Nonviolence works because, as Gene Sharp explains, "the exercise of power depends on the consent of the ruled who, by withdrawing that consent, can control and even destroy the power of their opponent". A democratic conception of politics is essential for Sharp's understanding of political jiu-jitsu. Sharp explains that repression of nonviolent resisters ends up rebounding against repressive violence and thus weakening its power. "By remaining nonviolent while continuing the struggle, the resisters can improve their own power position". Sharp identifies three ways that nonviolent resistance to repressive political power works:

1. by alienating support for the repressive power among the "usual supporters";
2. by increasing the power and support of the resistance movement; and
3. by turning third parties against the repressive group.

In general, when repressive political power uses violence against nonviolent resisters, this causes repressive power to expose itself, as Sharp says, "in the worst possible light". This may cause defections from among the dominant group even including politicians who change parties, police who refuse to carry out orders, and mutinies in the military. It can lead members of the protesting party to increase their efforts, while encouraging others to join the effort and become more active in their protests. Sharp explains that "repression can legitimize the resistance movement" and that "repression can both increase the determination of the existing nonviolent resisters and may at times increase the number of resisters". And finally, third parties can be converted toward more active support of the protest movement: whether this is in the media, the domestic business community, or in the international community.

The idea of voluntary suffering and the strategies of nonviolent jiu-jitsu lead to a troubling question of strategy: does it serve the interests of a nonviolent protest movement to be attacked? It might seem that what the nonviolent protester wants is, in fact, to be attacked, since there are benefits to be obtained from responding to such attacks nonviolently. Critics of nonviolence might argue that this shows a kind of passive-aggressive hypocrisy in nonviolence, which manipulates an opponent into making an attack and then blames the attacker. Certainly, it would be better not to be attacked. It would be best if institutions were not repressive and if human rights were respected and social justice prevailed. But the strategies of nonviolence usually come into play in circumstances when this is not the case. Thus the defender of nonviolence can respond to the charge of hypocrisy by saying that they did not manipulate violent and repressive forces into attacking them; rather, they were merely exposing the repression and violence of an unjust status quo.

Principled and Pragmatic Nonviolence

Now that we have a preliminary idea of how nonviolence works, let's consider why one might opt to take up the techniques of nonviolence. An important point to make here is that one need not be a pacifist to practice nonviolence. Nonviolence can be chosen for strategic reasons even by those who are not committed to the idea that violence is wrong. An obvious reason not to use violence is because you lack weapons, opportunity, training, and support. This is one of the reasons that nonviolence is sometimes understood as the power of the powerless. This may mean that nonviolence is used as a matter of prudence by those who lack the capacity to emerge victorious from a violent conflict. Related to this are other prudential considerations about effectiveness. It is important to ask what works, what we can afford, what we are able to do, and what we are willing to risk. These kinds of questions are merely pragmatic —they involve practical, strategic, and prudential concerns.

This sort of reasoning is quite different from a more principled commitment to nonviolence. Sometimes the principled commitment to nonviolence is called "pacifism". But pacifism is a complex idea, admitting different interpretations (as we discussed in a prior chapter). Some kinds of pacifism are merely opposed to war, which is massive and organized political violence. Anti-war pacifists may not, however, be opposed to violence in all circumstances. Thus, some anti-war protestors have used violence in their protests against war (as, for example, during the Vietnam era in American history). But others adopt a more thoroughgoing and comprehensive approach to pacifism and nonviolence.

Authors such as Barry Gan and Andrew Fitz-Gibbon have distinguished between "selective nonviolence" and "comprehensive nonviolence". Comprehensive nonviolence would be a kind of thoroughgoing or "absolute" pacifism, while selective nonviolence might be connected to what is sometimes called "contingent pacifism". For our purposes, let's focus on the distinction between principled/comprehensive and pragmatic/selective nonviolence.

Principled or comprehensive nonviolence rests upon a fundamental claim about the wrongness of violence and the "rightness" of nonviolence. There will even be differences among those who adhere to principled nonviolence. Some absolute pacifists may view the prohibition on violence as a law that can never be violated. Others may think that while there is a general rule against violence, there are conflicting principles, which are also of value. From this perspective, the rule against violence is not absolute: nonviolence is preferred but not absolutely required. One non-absolute version of principled nonviolence might be called "prima facie" nonviolence. A prima facie commitment to nonviolence would say that we ought to use nonviolent methods, unless there is some overriding duty not to do so.

Pragmatic or selective nonviolence does not rest upon any fundamental claim about the morality of nonviolence. Instead, pragmatic nonviolence is focused on the question of what works. From a pragmatic perspective, the answer to that question depends upon a variety of factors, especially the issue of what our goals are, what tools are available to us, and what the current situation looks like. Goals are usually selected for moral and political reasons: a moral and political framework helps us to determine the ends we pursue. But a pragmatic approach to seeking these ends is often willing to use a variety of different tools, so long as they are effective. The question of effectiveness depends upon empirical and historical factors, which help determine both which tools are available and which methods are likely to be effective.

There is also an important question here about how we coordinate short-term and long-term goals. Advocates of violence are often focused on short-term effectiveness, while advocates of nonviolence tend to be more focused on the longer term and the bigger picture. Consider how this works in an ordinary domestic case. A parent may be tempted to spank their child to teach a quick lesson. There will likely be an immediate effect. But the advocate of nonviolent parenting will point out that lessons can also be taught nonviolently, while also warning about the long-term repercussions of a parenting style that involves violence. These repercussions include the risk of escalation and abuse, as well as the general tone that is set by the resort to violence. It is easy to expand beyond this example to think about different approaches to criminal justice, styles of social protest, and issues such as terrorism and political violence. The advocate of violence will argue that violence can be effective in such cases; the advocate of nonviolence will say that what appears to work in the short run often ends up producing worse outcomes in the long run.

Pragmatic accounts may lead us to think that "the end justifies the means". That idea is usually thought to imply that anything goes in pursuit of our ends —and is often used to justify violence. But the question of whether "anything goes" must be supplemented by careful study of what actually works —in both the short-term and the long-term. Those who defend nonviolence on pragmatic grounds will argue that nonviolence is more effective than violence. But there remain a variety of open question about effectiveness. Effective to what extent? How lasting are its effects? And what are the risks associated with it?

A more comprehensive defense of nonviolence will offer a theory about short- and long-term effects, about the political and spiritual risks of violence, and about the transformational power of nonviolence. Comprehensive nonviolence tends to reject the idea that the end justifies the means. Rather, defenders of principled nonviolence tend to hold that ends and means must be coordinated. Some defenders of nonviolence put this quite strongly. Gandhi said, "I believe means and ends to be intimately interconnected. That is, a good end can never be achieved through bad means". King said: "Ends and means must cohere… For in the long run, we must see that the end represents the means in process and the idea in the making. In other words, we cannot believe, or we cannot go with the idea that the end justifies the means because the end is preexistent in the means". Michael Nagler said, "means and ends are one and indivisible". A very strong commitment to nonviolence follows from this way of thinking. If the means and the ends must cohere, then the use of violence as a means would undermine any nonviolent goals we might be pursuing.

Sometimes this is stated in a way that appeals to a kind of metaphysical principle of harmony, or something like the law of karma. Martin Luther King famously said, "the arc of the moral universe is long, but it bends toward justice". Such an idea makes sense from within King's religious point of view. From this perspective, the claim is made that violent means used in pursuit of nonviolent ends can wind up backfiring because of some kind of cosmic structure of cause and effect. This could also be grounded in empirical work in psychology and sociology, which shows how violence produces backlash, resistance, and tends toward escalation. There is also a normative point to be made here, which is that our actions model and enact the values we pursue. There usually is a connection between means and ends in political movements and ideologies. Liberal-democratic movements are grounded in basic ideas about respect for human rights, the importance of the rule of law, and the need for nonviolent transfers of power. Violent movements risk violating those kinds of values. If a violent political movement were to come to power, it's methodology would be at odds with the prevailing values of democracy. Violent movements are more likely to become oppressive and authoritarian when they succeed and come to power. Let's turn to the question of democracy next.

Democracy and Nonviolence

The idea coordinating means and ends is also a central idea for democratic politics. If we value human rights, the rule of law, and peaceful transfers of power as ends to be pursued in political life, then we ought to use correlated democratic means in pursuit of those ends. Those democratic means will be nonviolent.

Said differently, nonviolent means are the best tools we have for cultivating democracy and peace. This is not an absolute truth, although there is substantial empirical evidence pointing toward this general tendency. At the end of their long historical account of successful nonviolent movements, Ackerman and DuVall explain, "if the channel to democracy has been navigated with the pilot of a nonviolent movement at its helm, the nation's ability to sustain democracy will be greater than if no strategy for popular resistance has led the way". More recently, Hallward and Norman concluded, after their extensive review of the literature, "democratic, nonviolent means are more likely to result in more democratic ends". Bartkowski explains that nonviolence tends to result in free and more durable democratic transitions, while armed struggle depends upon hierarchical and secretive leadership and processes, which result in undemocratic outcomes.

Now the term "democracy" is —like the term "pacifism"— one that can be interpreted in various ways. The idea of democracy discussed here is one that is intimately connected with nonviolence. Governments that call themselves "democracies" can be warlike. If democracy is understood etymologically, it means simply "rule of the people". But "the people" can be warlike. They can also choose to oppress others who are not considered full-fledged members of "the people": for example, women, foreigners, or slaves. Democracies can contain internal disputes and wind up in civil wars. And a democratic polity can employ violence in domestic affairs (in policing, for example, or with the use of the death penalty).

But if democracy is understood as requiring the consent of the governed, something else emerges, which is a notion of political power that can be disrupted when the people withdraw their consent. This idea is developed under the general idea of "the social contract", which is central to modern political theory as developed in various ways by Thomas Hobbes, John Locke, Jean-Jacques Rousseau, Immanuel Kant, and in the twentieth century by John Rawls. The social contract theory is not nonviolent: it has been the source of arguments in favor of violent political revolution. John Locke said, "all peaceful beginnings of government have been laid in the consent of the people". But this implies that when there is conquest or when government is instituted which violates this notion of consent, then a revolution can be justified. Thomas Jefferson and the American revolutionaries said, in the American Declaration of Independence:

> Governments are instituted among Men, deriving their just powers from the consent of the governed.... Whenever any Form of Government becomes destructive of these ends, it is the right of the People to alter or to abolish it, and to institute new Government.

Locke and Jefferson established the right of people to resist, including the right to engage in a violent revolution.

The proponents of nonviolence assume the modern democratic idea of political legitimacy as consent. But they add that protests and insurrections should be nonviolent. And in advocating nonviolence, they also take a critical stand toward the use of violence in ordinary or normal politics, including structural violence that is found within modern, liberal democracies. Modern *states* (whether democratic or otherwise) contain a monopoly on the use of violence —and so are not actually nonviolent. For this reason, the ideal of democracy that is most closely connected with the ideal of nonviolence might actually be a kind of anarchism. We'll return to this point in a moment.

But let's consider the connection between state-centered liberal-democracy and nonviolence. The idea that democracies tend to be more peaceful has come to be accepted as a truism in the scholarship of international relations. The so-called "democratic peace theory" holds that democratic states do not go to war against one another. A related idea, "the capitalist peace theory", holds that violence among nations decreases when prosperity grows and when there are substantial trading relationships between nations. One could argue that market relationships are basically nonviolent: we engage one another nonviolently when we freely trade with one another. Furthermore, with regard to domestic politics in liberal-democratic states, the idea is that when there is respect for human rights, respect for the rule of law, and a commitment to peaceful transfers of power, domestic political life is less violent.

These ideas have led Rummel, for example, to reach several basic conclusions that are linked under his general claim that "democracy is a method of nonviolence". Rummel maintains:

1. Well-established democracies do not make war on and rarely commit lesser violence against each other.
2. The more two nations are democratic, the less likely war or lesser violence between them.
3. The more a nation is democratic, the less severe its overall foreign violence.
4. The more democratic a nation, the less likely it will have domestic collective violence.
5. The more democratic a nation, the less its democide (i.e., mass murder/genocide).

Rummel's approach is grounded in empirical study and historical fact. A similar approach has been developed by Steven Pinker, who has built upon Rummel's work (and other empirical accounts). Pinker reaches a similar conclusion about the relationship between liberal-democratic values, enlightenment, modernity, and peace. Explaining this idea as it was developed in the writing of Immanuel Kant around the turn of the eighteenth century, Pinker explains,

"Democracies are unlikely to fight each other, Kant argued, for two reasons. One is that democracy is a form of government that by design... is built around nonviolence... More important, democracies tend to avoid wars because the benefits of war go to a country's leaders whereas the costs are paid by its citizens". This last point is related to the idea that, in a democracy, the government rules by consent of the governed. Kant supposed that if ordinary people were asked if they wanted to go to war (and also to pay for it with their tax dollars), they would choose not to fight.

The real world is more complicated than this. There are numerous examples of democratic citizens supporting war (say, for example, in the initial popularity of the American wars against Afghanistan and Iraq). We might add to the mix here the idea that citizens must also be "enlightened", as Kant might put it. In order to make wise decisions about war, citizens must be educated about the morality of war, the costs of war, the causes of war, and the likelihood of success. And old-fashioned nationalism must give way to a more enlightened sort of cosmopolitanism.

There is more to be said about these issues. A complete account would explore the issues of racism, inequality and exploitation within democratic states, as well as the history of slavery and colonialism in the genealogy of modern liberal-democracies. There is remaining structural violence within so-called democratic states. This is, for example, what has motivated Black Lives Matter protests organized in opposition to the use of violence against Black people in the United States. We might also want to dig further into questions about the ways that the United States has proved to be somewhat of an anomaly, since the U.S. possesses the world's largest military budget, has used torture, continues to employ the death penalty, and so on. Perhaps the U.S. is not as democratic as it thinks it is (if a commitment to nonviolence is thought to be one of the hallmarks of democracy). Or it might be that there is something else about the U.S. —say, its role as a superpower or its deep history of racism— that helps explain this anomaly.

Now let's look a bit more carefully at the question of peaceful transfers of power, as this will help prepare the ground for our subsequent discussion of extra-institutional politics. Ideally in a democracy, when one politician or his/her party loses power, they will peacefully make way for another politician and party. This is among the most basic premises of democracy. The electoral system is supposed to result in a peaceful transfer of power. It is this process that allows citizens to feel that their voices matter and that the government is grounded upon the consent of the governed. Political violence undermines this process and destroys the most fundamental assumption of democracy.

There are non-democratic ways that peaceful transfers of power can occur. A monarch can pass power on to his son. A group of plutocrats can distribute power among themselves. Or a dictator can handpick his successor. But it is the violent changes of power that provide the most significant challenge: military coups, foreign invasions, and so on. Violent transitions violate the democratic ideal. If a person or party comes to power through violence, the regime will lack democratic legitimacy. It will not be able to govern with the consent of the governed and will thus have to become violent and oppressive in order to coerce the citizenry to conform and obey.

Many so-called democracies were born out of violence. The United States provides an example. The United States was formed by way of a violent revolution. The country expanded through the use of colonial violence, which expropriated land, exterminated native peoples, and maintained a slave economy. And the "union" was preserved by way of a bloody civil war. This example shows that it is not always true that violence prevents the birth of democracy —if we consider the U.S. a democracy.

And yet, revisionist historians interested in nonviolence have argued that the real birth of the United States occurred before the violence of the revolution, in the nonviolent movements of the 1760s and 1770s. This included American colonial resistance to "taxation without representation" and the symbolic protest of the "Boston Tea Party". Gene Sharp has referred to this as part of what he calls "the American colonial nonviolent revolution". Throughout this period there was systematic noncooperation with British authorities including boycotts, work stoppages, and so on. There were also demonstrations, pamphleteering, and the development of self-reliant production connected to an American refusal to buy British products. This included extensive participation by women, who helped to spin American cloth (and thus established independence from British imports) and who participated in protests, boycotts, and so on. All of this created a growing sense of independence, which led to the development of "parallel institutions". These methods were not systematically developed —they grew organically as circumstances unfolded. But these are among the paradigmatic strategies of nonviolent social movements. These are strategies of noncooperation, nonconsumption, nonimportation, nonexportation. Along with the creation of parallel institutions, these are obviously strategies that also encourage independence. A polity becomes self-reliant through this nonviolent work.

Similar ideas were part of the Indian independence movement led by Gandhi. Instead of George Washington leading an army, however, the Indian movement was led by a proponent of nonviolence. Nonetheless, there was also violence in the Indian case —both violence inflicted on the movement by the British and the violent unravelling of Indian society during and after the time of independence and partition. The violence of this time appalled Gandhi. But it continued and continues today, with Pakistan and India —two nuclear-armed nations— engaged in a conflict that has lasted for decades. One of the ironies of history is that India, the land of Gandhi, has given birth to two nuclear states. This becomes more ironic when we learn that the code name for the Indian nuclear program was "Smiling Buddha".

Independence in the era of nation-states requires a people to build up and support a military force. But advocates of nonviolence insist that the goal should be self-reliance and independence rather than the pursuit of power for its own sake and escalation of violent conflict. The goal of a democratic liberation movement is not to empower the military and consolidate the monopoly of violence (as Weber put it). Instead, advocates of nonviolence and democracy understand power differently. Nonviolent democratic movements usually involve a broad and inclusive set of actors, including farmers, shopkeepers, women, children, and the aged. Everyone can get involved in a campaign of noncooperation or a boycott. But military action is usually restricted to able-bodied men. Another difference has to do with structures of command and obedience. Military power requires hierarchical control and a kind of unquestioning obedience. But nonviolent protest tends to be more decentralized and less conformist, including an open receptivity to the creative and spontaneous acts of individuals. For a nonviolent movement to be successful, it must be coordinated, sustained, and strategic. But the way that nonviolent movements accomplish this is democratic, involving more of a grass-roots or bottom-up system than a top-down or hierarchical system. The result of these differences in strategy and organization will be seen in the way that power is organized after the revolution is accomplished. Violent, militant movements will tend to reproduce elitism, hierarchy, centralization, and violence after they come to power. Nonviolent, democratic movements will tend to focus on inclusivity, decentralization, and broad participation as both the means of creating change and the ends or goals that are being pursued.

Anarchism and Extra-Institutional Politics

Military coups and violent revolutions occur regularly throughout the history of civilization. Sometimes history appears to be an account of violence insofar as history focuses primarily on spectacular violent events like wars and revolutions. While there are examples of successful violent revolutions, in many cases the arrival of militancy often spells the end of democracy. This is a lesson as old as ancient Rome. It can be seen in the Napoleonic era and in the rise of fascism and totalitarianism in the twentieth century. When a violent revolution occurs, democracy is at risk because, as Arendt has explained, violence and terror are one-sided: they lack the power of legitimacy and consent. When a political structure is instituted by violence and supported primarily by violence or the threat of violence, it must become increasingly violent in order to maintain its power. The violence that is typical of the political structure (i.e., the violence of the state) often provokes violence among those revolutionaries who reject the state's authority. Nonviolent protest offers an alternative to the ongoing dialectic of political violence. This alternative often includes a critique of state violence that verges upon anarchism.

A significant problem for nonviolence and democracy is that states are often the greatest purveyors of violence. Modern states typically have a violent birth and grow by consolidating and centralizing violent power. Nuclear weapons and genocide represent terrible culminations of this development. Nonviolence, of course, points in a different direction. The advocates of nonviolence have often been critical of state-violence. Indeed, the strategies of nonviolence often work by exposing the violence of the state through the kind of political jiu-jitsu described by Gene Sharp. When the state cracks down on nonviolent protesters, the state's use of violence serves to delegitimize its power.

This is why there is a close connection between nonviolence and the critique of state violence that is known as anarchism. Anarchism is another complex term. Most basically, it implies a rejection of centralized and hierarchical political power. And since states use violence in defense of their centralized power, anarchists have often connected their criticism of state violence to a more positive affirmation of nonviolence. This critique of state power and state violence is connected to a general commitment to the autonomy of the individual and a defense of democracy, although in this case democracy is understood directly as "people power" and not as a form of state-centered governance. This is not to say that all anarchists are nonviolent. Indeed, the image of anarchism in the popular mind is often associated with violence. But anarchists have often been critical of violence; and more than a few of the advocates of nonviolence have been sympathetic to anarchism.

Leo Tolstoy provides a paradigm example. Tolstoy grounding his anarchist and pacifist ideas in his own idiosyncratic interpretation of the Christian gospels. Tolstoy explained that his goal was "the abolition of the organization of government formed to do violence". He thought that this would facilitate "a juster and more reasonable social organization, needing no violence". This sort of thinking had an influence on Gandhi, who named one of his first cooperative communities Tolstoy Farm. Gandhi thought that, in theory at least, a perfect state would be "enlightened anarchy", which he described as a state in which "everyone is his own ruler". He also said, "the ideally non-violent State will be an ordered anarchy. That state will be the best governed which is governed the least". This idea echoes one found in the famous essay on "Civil Disobedience", written by American transcendentalist author Henry David Thoreau. Thoreau's call for civil disobedience was built upon those kinds of acts of noncooperation and disobedience that occurred during the nonviolent phase of the America revolution, as we discussed above.

There are a number of other authors who link anarchism and nonviolence. The French theologian Jacques Ellul said simply, "By anarchy I mean first an absolute rejection of violence". The religious basis of this view is made clear by Ellul, Tolstoy, and Gandhi. But one need not be an other-worldly saint to understand the problem of state power and violence. One of the significant problems raised by anarchist critics of violence is that states ask and even demand (in the case of conscript armies) that citizens kill on their behalf. And the tax dollars of citizens support the army and its killing (and indicate a kind of consent to this kind of violence). But if killing and violence are wrong, as the proponent of nonviolence believes, then the state is wrong to kill and to make such a demand upon its citizens. This leads Robert Holmes to point out that nonviolentism, as he calls it, is closely connected to anarchism.

Of course, as critics of anarchism have long pointed out, to call for the abolition of the state in theory is one thing, but to bring this about in reality would likely require substantial violence. And one wonders whether anarchy would be successful at limiting and preventing violence. The proponents of modern liberal-democratic states typically argue that the state offers the best hope for minimizing violence by defending human rights, adhering to the rule of law, and ensuring peaceful transfers of power.

Modern liberal-democratic states are imperfect. But they are, at least, a step in the direction of reducing violence. The hope of many nonviolent activists around the world is to make the transition from authoritarian and colonial regimes in order to enjoy the benefits of democracy. And within modern democratic states, nonviolent movements continue to demand that these states live up to their promise.

To make that demand —to demand that a state lives up to ethical standards— often requires the emergence of extra-institutional politics. In some cases, there are ordinary legal channels for challenging state power. You can run for office or support a party in order to make change in a democratic country. In some countries, citizens can sue the state for violating their rights. To operate within the legal and political framework is in fact a kind of nonviolence: voting, organizing, and running for office are among the most basic nonviolent techniques for creating social change. But in some cases, this is often either not possible (in authoritarian regimes) or ineffective (when structural violence prevents even democratic states from fulfilling their promise of equal justice under the law). Extra-institutional politics emerges as a challenge to the legal and political system.

Extra-institutional nonviolent democratic movements involve a variety of nonviolent actions, including both strategies of non-cooperation and the creation of alternative institutions. Protests and revolutions require strategic action directly against repressive power. But successful nonviolent movements for democratic change must also create structures and systems that exist outside of the channels of mainstream and officially sanctioned politics.

Indeed, these structures and systems often exist in society prior to the outbreak of active nonviolent campaigns. They are found in churches, in political parties, in fraternal organizations, in labor unions, in civic groups, in universities, and so on. There are a variety of ways that people organize themselves outside of political life —in what is often called "civil society". The organizations of civil society are crucial for bringing people together in extra-institutional politics. A strike or a rally needs some social group to organize it. Sometimes these groups can emerge in the midst of a struggle. But often they precede it. In the case of nonviolent protests in Russia in 1905, labor organizations and religious leaders were instrumental. In the American civil rights movement of the 1960s, churches were crucial. In resistance to the Soviet system in the 60s and again in the 1980s in Poland, Czechoslovakia, and East Germany, the movement involved labor organizations, groups of artists, and religion. Students have often been in the forefront of these kinds of activities, since students are easily organized at universities. In the Arab Spring during the early 2010s, the Occupy Wall Street protests of that time, and in contemporary Black Lives Matter protests, the added element of social media came into play.

And even when protests and social movements appear to be the spontaneous acts of heroic individuals, there is often much more to the story in terms of social organization. Rosa Parks, who famously sat down on the bus in Montgomery, Alabama, was selected and trained to do her part in instigating the movement. She was a member of the National Association for the Advancement of Colored People (NAACP), which helped to coordinate and pay for her legal defense. After she played her part, a whole system of organized support moved into action, spreading the news, supporting those who boycotted the buses, and generally working to facilitate the movement. A similar story can be told about the Arab Spring protests. In Tunisia, when Mohamed Bouazizi set himself on fire in 2010 in a protest against the regime of Tunisian President Zine El Abidine Ben Ali, there was a whole network already in place that was prepared to step up and transform this spontaneous outpouring of frustration into the movement that became the Arab Spring. And Bouazizi's act was not unprecedented. There had been protests against Ben Ali in the past, just as African Americans had protested inequality before Rosa Parks. But in cases like these, something clicks. An individual rises to the occasion and gives heart to a movement. Sometimes this occurs without the individual in question even playing an active role in the movement, as when protests erupted after the killing of George Floyd by police in 2020. Sometimes a mass movement occurs in response to a catalyzing event: but some organization and coordination is required in advance for these spontaneous outbursts to occur. The Black Lives Matter movement was already active before George Floyd was murdered.

The work of "extra-institutional" politics is complex and it overlaps with institutional efforts. Institutional political processes involve voting, running for office, attending town-hall meetings with politicians, raising money for political campaigns, proposing legislation, and filing lawsuits. On the other hand, extra-institutional action involves individuals and groups who engage in what is sometimes called "direct action". Rather than operating within normal channels of the political process, extra-institutional direct action occurs elsewhere: in the streets, at public demonstrations, on social-media, and on the picket line. There is no firm line of distinction between institutional and extra-institutional methods of promoting social and political change. And often people, parties, and groups engage in both forms: staging protests, strikes, and demonstrations while also lobbying politicians, proposing legislation, running for office, and voting. As we have already discussed, democratic political life is nonviolent: voting, writing to your representative, and speaking out at a town hall meeting are forms of nonviolent action. When these actions do not bear fruit, people turn to extra-institutional methods.

6. Young boy shouting on a megaphone in a protest.

There is no necessary connection between extra-institutional political methods and nonviolence. Indeed, terrorism is an extra-institutional method, as is sabotage, vandalism, and property destruction. Proponents of nonviolence reject violent tactics. Most obviously, nonviolent activists would reject terrorism, which is a violent attack on persons. Sabotage, vandalism, and property destruction are less clearly violent —depending on how we define these actions. There is a continuum here, which involves judgment about circumstances, harms, and so on. On the one hand, some acts of sabotage can create substantial harm to persons; and property destruction can also cause harm (for example, when bystanders are harmed). On the other hand, there is a kind of symbolic property destruction and vandalism that harms no one. Consider, for example, Catholic peace activists known as the Plowshares movement. The name comes from the Biblical verse about beating swords into plowshares (Isaiah 2:4). Members of this group trespass on military sites, spill their own blood, and symbolically strike weapons or facilities with hammers. In 2018, seven Plowshares protesters were arrested at a U.S. military establishment in Georgia, where they protested against nuclear weapons. This was a group of mostly senior citizens: it included a 79-year-old nun, a 70-year-old priest, and one 62-year-old protestor, Martha Hennessey, who is Dorothy Day's granddaughter. These protestors were found guilty of conspiracy, destruction of government property, trespassing, and depredation in 2019.

This example shows us one of the reasons that people turn to extra-institutional direct action. It seems impossible to change the military and nuclear strategies of the United States without employing extra-institutional methods: the political establishment is too tightly wedded to militarism. So activists seeking to make an impact turn to extra-institutional means. The same impetus that leads some to take up terrorism is what leads others to employ the methods of nonviolent social protest, i.e., a sense that the ordinary institutions of political life are corrupt, unjust, or unresponsive. Ideally, the political system would be responsive, rational, and just. In some versions of the ideal democracy, the ordinary structures of political life should be sufficient to defend justice and the interests of citizens. But in the non-ideal world, it is often the case that even in supposedly democratic states there is need for ongoing nonviolent protest. Indeed, some democratic states enshrine this in their constitutional principles by explicitly protecting freedom of religion, freedom of speech, freedom of the press, the right to assemble, and the right to petition the government. In the U.S., these rights are included in the First Amendment to the U.S. Constitution, along with freedom of religion, which can be seen as safeguarding the possibility of extra-institutional and nonviolent protest.

The idea of extra-institutional direct action has often been closely related to anarchism: if the state and its institutions are corrupt, unjust, and illegitimate, then there is no reason to adhere to institutional methods or to hope that they will be effective. We mentioned Dorothy Day above, who founded and led the Catholic Worker movement. She was a committed pacifist and anarchist who devoted her life to serving the poor and opposing militarism. In 1954 in an essay written in opposition to the development of the hydrogen bomb she said:

> When it is said that we disturb people too much by the words pacifism and anarchism, I can only think that people need to be disturbed, that their consciences need to be aroused, that they do indeed need to look into their work, and study new techniques of love and poverty and suffering for each other.

Dorothy Day was jailed during social protests. She opposed both the First World War and the Second World War. She refused to pay taxes. And she never voted, despite the fact that she was arrested and jailed in 1917 for participating in the women's suffrage movement. She explained in 1967: "I went to jail in Washington, upholding the rights of political prisoners. An anarchist then as I am now, I have never used the vote that the women won by their demonstrations". Day provides an example of a person committed to nonviolent social change, whose emphasis is entirely on extra-institutional action. Her efforts were intended to show that there is something wrong in a system that locks nuns and priests away for nonviolently protesting against nuclear weapons and which imprisons women who want to vote.

Methods of Nonviolence including Boycotts and Civil Disobedience

It is sometimes difficult to draw a clear line between violent and nonviolent action. This effort is made more difficult by the fact that there are quite a number of techniques and methods of nonviolent action. We mentioned at the outset that Gene Sharp identified nearly 200 techniques of nonviolence and that these can be grouped in three general categories.

- Symbolic protest and persuasion (for example, letter writing);
- Non-cooperation (for example, work slow-downs); and
- Intervention (for example, civil disobedience).

We have discussed much of this in passing throughout the book. But let's consider a couple of techniques here in more detail —boycotts and civil disobedience— because these provide good examples of the challenges and opportunities created by the array of nonviolent techniques.

Economic Boycotts. One typical approach is to boycott products or profit-making activities —so-called economic boycotts. There are a variety of examples: "boycott and divest" movements directed at South Africa or Israel, the grape boycott organized by Cesar Chavez and the United Farm Workers, the Rosa Parks-inspired bus boycott in Montgomery, Alabama, and Gandhi-led boycotts of British products in India. These actions aim to make a strategic point by undermining the profit of those who control the levers of power. Some boycotts have been effective: Chavez's grape boycott worked to raise consciousness about the injustice afflicting farm laborers. But some are not: the attempt to force change in Israel through various boycotts has mostly been unsuccessful. There are a number of circumstantial factors that influence the effectiveness of a boycott including how unified and organized the boycott is, how much damage is done through the boycott, the amount of opposition and resistance to the boycott, and how long the boycott is able to sustain itself. But the further issue is the question of harm done by boycotts. In some cases, it turns out that those who are harmed are those on the bottom end of the social and political hierarchy. A boycott against a poor authoritarian regime is likely not to do much harm to the ruling elites; rather, it will cause harm to those the boycott is intending to help. This is why scholars such as Johan Galtung have suggested that boycotts may be a form of violence.

Political Boycotts. Now consider another form of boycott, what we might call a boycott of political life, which involves a refusal to vote (an election boycott) and also a refusal to participate in the ordinary political life of the nation. This might include a boycott of patriotic celebrations, commemorations, parades, and so on —including refusing to salute the flag. At the international level it might manifest itself as a refusal to negotiate with, trade with, or recognize the legitimacy of a foreign government. Political boycotts do not seem violent: they don't risk causing harm to the vulnerable in the way that economic boycotts do. But they present a difficulty that is connected with the point we made earlier about the connections between nonviolence and democracy. Democratic political action, especially elections, seems to be both symbolically and practically important. The practical point is that in order to effect social and political change it makes sense to vote for candidates that advance your agenda. The symbolic point is this: it seems that you should participate in democratic practice if it is democracy that you are aiming for. However, the circumstances matter. The corrupt electoral systems of authoritarian regimes are not truly democratic. Does it make sense to vote when there is only one candidate and the election is rigged by the state/party apparatus? In such cases voting is a largely symbolic act, which makes refusal to participate symbolic as well. In such a system your vote (or non-vote) will have no practical impact. In not voting in such a case, you withdraw your allegiance and make a symbolic protest. There are complexities here that depend upon the circumstances. Does it make sense to vote in an American Presidential election when there are only two viable parties and the electoral college system seems to undermine the value of the popular vote? What if a protest vote (or a non-vote) results in an electoral outcome that makes things worse? And, at the international level, what if non-recognition of a foreign state results in long-term animosity, provokes instability, or undermines efforts at developing global justice? Practical and symbolic considerations will have to be accounted for in cases such as these.

We saw above that Dorothy Day never voted: her pacifist and anarchist critique of the state seemed to cause her to withdraw her allegiance and opt out of institutional politics. But Day was also active in the women's suffrage movement. Perhaps this is paradoxical. Or maybe there is a difference between having the right to vote and finding politicians and policies that are worth voting for.

Civil Disobedience. Civil disobedience is perhaps one of the most famous of the strategies of nonviolent action. We saw above that Dorothy Day practiced civil disobedience and spent time in jail. Martin Luther King Jr. was jailed, where he wrote his famous "Letter for Birmingham Jail". Gandhi was jailed. And before him, Henry David Thoreau went to jail for refusing to pay taxes. Tax protest is among the strategies of nonviolent action. But evading tax-payment (because you are a selfish and greedy criminal) is not the same as being willing to go to jail as a result of refusing to pay taxes out of a conscientious desire for justice. The law may treat you the same in both cases. But proponents of civil disobedience don't disobey to get away with a crime. They allow themselves to be arrested in order to call attention to the question of the legitimacy of the law.

In fact, civil disobedience has been defended as expressing a kind of loyalty or fidelity to law: either to the natural law that is thought to provide the basis for civil law or to the democratic principles of the constitutional system. Martin Luther King Jr. explains civil disobedience in terms of the natural law that transcends the civil law, appealing to ideas found in Augustine and Aquinas. He says that in breaking the law, the conscientious protestor expresses respect for the higher law.

While King situates his approach in the natural law tradition, others explain civil disobedience in terms of democratic and constitutional law, more closely associated with the social contract theory. This is how John Rawls, the influential American political theorist, explains and defends it. Rawls is not known primarily as a proponent of nonviolence. But he is one of the important defenders of liberal-democratic political theory; and he defended the right of conscientious refusal and civil disobedience based upon liberal-democratic principles. Rawls suggests that civil disobedience is an important part of liberal-democratic politics, so long as it occurs within the general framework of "fidelity to law". Rawls suggests that civil disobedience appeals to the sense of justice of the majority, as well as the basic values embodied in the constitutional system. He defines civil disobedience as a "public, nonviolent conscientious yet political act contrary to law usually done with the aim of bringing about a change in the law or policies of the government". This means that civil disobedience is a "political act", guided by a shared or common conception of justice. It is not then the willful actions of criminals and relativists who simply do not like the status quo. As a political act, civil disobedience is a "public" kind of law-breaking. It is not done in secret or in sneaky ways. Indeed, the point of civil disobedience is not to "get away" with a crime. Rather, the goal is to break the law in public and even to get arrested, as a way of making a political point. And as a nonviolent act, civil disobedience is not a threat to public order, security, or safety. Rawls explains, "while it may warn and admonish, it is not itself a threat".

In conclusion, let's note that civil disobedience may occur in various forms. It may directly violate an unjust law. This is what happened, for example, when Black civil rights protestors broke segregationist laws during the American civil rights movement. But civil disobedience can also be used in ways that are less directly related to the laws that are being protested. Sometimes, civil disobedience occurs in situations that are set up deliberately in order to provoke arrest. Thus protestors and demonstrators may violate the conditions of a parade permit. In such a case, the resulting arrest has nothing to do with the law or policy that is being protested. Consider, for example, an environmental group that gets arrested for an illegal march or demonstration that blocks traffic: their real focus is the environmental issues and not issues related to parade permits and traffic laws. In general, the strategic goal is to break the law in order to provoke a response by the police, to capture the attention of the public, and thus to draw attention and gain solidarity and sympathy.

Conclusion: Pragmatic Effectiveness vs. Deep Transformation

As we conclude this chapter and this book, let's return to the question of how and why these techniques work and the distinction between pragmatic and principled nonviolence. On the one hand there are practical effects of nonviolent protest and campaigns of noncooperation. Nonviolent noncooperation can be effective —both in the short- and long-term. A strike or work stoppage has the immediate result of halting production. And strikes can induce long-term change in the case of negotiated settlements and mediation of disputes. There are instances of nonviolent noncooperation effectively changing political and legal systems: in Gandhi's campaigns, in the American Civil Rights movement, and in the revolutionary transformations in Europe at the end of the Cold War. Such activities can even be effective in response to invading armies and foreign occupation, as seen in Czechoslovakian resistance to Soviet power in 1968 or in the case of Danish noncooperation with the occupying Nazi power.

So it is clear that nonviolence can work at the practical level. It has the power to force negotiations and accommodations. Perhaps that is sufficient. But the most celebrated advocates of nonviolence often have something further in mind when they invoke the power of nonviolence: not merely coercion but also persuasion and even conversion. In addition to effective resistance to injustice and progressive development in the legal system, advocates of nonviolence often imagine a more profound social transformation. In addition to using nonviolence as an effective technique, they envision it as fostering a radical transformation in social ontology. The most radical proponents of nonviolence want a conversion of the heart that would transform society from top to bottom.

In our previous discussion of social ontology, we mentioned lofty ideals about brotherhood, love, compassion, and so on. Gandhi, King, and others believe that nonviolence has the capacity to convert and transform. This aspiration is understandable, even if conversion may be too much to ask in many cases. Danish nonviolent resistance was not likely to convert many Nazis. The Nazis may have grudgingly accommodated themselves to Danish noncooperation. But there are complexities of psychology, social identity, and culture that are at play in the life of a committed Nazi, which make it difficult to imagine a change of heart happening as the result of encountering Danish nonviolent resistance.

And yet… long term social transformation seems to be more likely when nonviolence is employed. The way to change "hearts and minds", as the saying goes, is through what is called "soft power" in international relations and foreign policy. Jonathan Schell has explained how this has worked in concrete cases, including in the early days of the French Revolution. The famous event known as the "storming of the Bastille" on July 14, 1789, which has been commemorated since then as the moment of French liberation, provides a surprising lesson in nonviolence. The march to the Bastille began as a nonviolent protest involving unarmed men, women, and children on July 12. After the French military assaulted the nonviolent protesters, the protesters armed themselves: it was escalation by the state that incited the uprising. And after a fight that killed 100 people, the revolutionaries finally took the Bastille as the guards surrendered. In Schell's account, the early and nearly bloodless success of the revolutionaries was the result of "winning the hearts and minds" of the opposition, who were no longer willing to defend the old regime. Schell explains that a revolution of hearts and minds is the key to successful revolution.

This echoes Gene Sharp's claims about the importance of consent. Consent can evaporate quickly, especially when there is solidarity and sympathy with those who protest. But as is well-known with regard to the French Revolution, violence did not end with the storming of the Bastille. A decade of terror followed, featuring the blood-soaked guillotine and eventually leading to Napoleon's coup and war with the rest of Europe.

This reminds us that the question of conversion and transformation requires substantially more than an initial act of heroism (whether violent or nonviolent). Long-term social and political transformation requires an effort that extends beyond any given generation. It is the product of a changed political structure, developments in culture including religion, and ongoing efforts to educate and enlighten. This returns us to our discussion of institutional and extra-institutional means of social transformation. It is not enough simply to take to the streets in nonviolent protest. A nonviolent movement aiming to create a more loving, truthful, and just world will also seek to transform the legal structure, and to build lasting cultural institutions. It will seek to transform religion, civil society, and economics and build a culture of peace. It will seek to transform family life and gender relationships in a way that promotes nonviolence. It will seek to educate youth about the power of nonviolence and the problem of violence. And so on.

In its broadest sense, the work of nonviolence is oriented toward developing what is called "positive peace". In the short term, the pragmatic methods of nonviolent protest can be effective. But the nonviolent imagination extends toward the creation of a world in which there is solidarity, justice, compassion, truth, and love. The proponents of nonviolence maintain that in order to create that world, we must employ means and methods that embody what we imagine. It is only by using the methods of nonviolence that we can hope to convert, transform, and build.

Let's conclude by returning to Gandhi, who called for a complete transformation of the way we live. In 1947, toward the end of his life, a month before he was assassinated, Gandhi responded to a question about what would need to happen for there to be world peace. He said the following:

> One must first look deeply into the causes of wars and seek ways to remove those causes. Wars in a large measure are fought over economic issues. If we give up selfishness and resolve to take the barest minimum for the satisfaction of our wants, there will be no occasion for wars. Unless there is a complete transformation in our economy and our style of life, peace will elude us, however hard we may strive for it.

Gandhi's advocacy for nonviolence is related to this vision of a way of life that is radically transformed. If peace is the goal, the method employed must be peaceful. From Gandhi's standpoint, the method of nonviolence transforms selfishness into simplicity, while giving us a vision of a new economy and style of life.

The nonviolent imagination provides a source of inspiration for creating a better world. Such a transformation is a project for the very long-term. We make progress in this direction when we understand how and why nonviolence works in the short run. We make progress when we cultivate a unity of means and ends. And we make progress when we develop the techniques of nonviolence and use them to build more inclusive and more just democracies. We make progress when we think critically about violence and understand the traditions and history of nonviolence. And we make progress when we realize that nonviolence gives us the power to build a better —more just, truthful, and loving— world.

Further reading

Ackerman, Peter and Jack DuVall (2000). *A Force More Powerful*. New York: St. Martin's Press.

Butler, Judith (2020). *The Force of Nonviolence*. London: Verso, 2020.

Chenoweth, Erica. & Stephan, Maria J. (2011). *Why Civil Resistance Works: The Strategic Logic of Nonviolent Conflict*. New York: Columbia University Press.

Cortright, David (2008). *Peace: A History of Movements and Ideas*. Cambridge: Cambridge University Press.

Fiala, Andrew (2018). *Transformative Pacifism*. London: Bloomsbury.

Fiala, Andrew, ed. (2018). *The Routledge Handbook of Pacifism and Nonviolence*. New York: Routledge.

Holmes, Robert L. (2013). *The Ethics of Nonviolence: Essays by Robert Holmes*. London: Bloomsbury.

Holmes, Robert L. (2017). *Pacifism: A Philosophy of Nonviolence*. London: Bloomsbury.

Kurlansky, Mark (2006). *Nonviolence: 25 Lessons From the History of a Dangerous Idea*. New York: Modern Library.

Sharp, Gene (1973). *The Politics of Nonviolent Action*. Boston: Porter Sargent.

Sharp, Gene (2013). *How Nonviolent Struggle Works*. Boston: The Albert Einstein Institution.

9 781949 845181

A Quick Immersion series

For more information visit our web site
www.quickimmersions.com